LOVE LIVES FOREVER
(FULL COLOR EDITION)

JoAnne Scannell Davis

Love Lives Forever

ARTWORK
BY
JEANNETTE STITELER

In Hearts and Souls and Verse

LOVE LIVES FOREVER

Published by JoAnne Scannell Davis
142 Dorwin Ave
Syracuse, NY 13205

jsdlegacy.com
davisjoannescannell@gmail.com

Interior artwork by Jeannette Stiteler
Edited by Pauline C. Harris
Cover artist: Mitxeran

First edition: 2023

ISBN 979-8-9874953-0-8 (E-Book)
ISBN 979-8-9874953-1-5 (Paperback, black & white edition)
ISBN 979-8-9874953-2-2 (Paperback, color edition)
ISBN 979-8-9874953-3-9 (Hardback, black & white edition)
ISBN 979-8-9874953-4-6 (Hardback, color edition)

Printed in the United States of America

Table of Contents

Table of Illustrations ix
Preface xiii
1. Prologue 1
2. The Owl 2
3. The Lion 3
4. Eleven Years and Fifty Days 4
5. Clouds 7
6. Life, the Universe and Everything – Philosophical 8
7. Life, the Universe and Everything – Personal 11
8. Tinkle Bell 12
9. God's Friends 15
10. Party Time 18
11. Sonnet to the Clouds 20
12. Wonderful Time 23
13. Pain's Prayer 25
14. The Villain 27
15. February Dreaming 29
16. Sensing Spring 31
17. Longing for Spring 33
18. Rejuvenation 34
19. Sequel to The Owl 36
20. My Decades Journal 38
21. Tis the Season 40
22. Sweet Home 42
23. Anticipation 44
24. Old Fashioned Summer 46
25. Remembered Freedom 49
26. For Alex 50
27. Truth Denied 51
28. Highway Wonder 52
29. The Odyssey 55
30. Contemplating Energy 56
31. The Fulfillment of Beauty 58
32. Monster Within 61
33. Changing of the Guard 62

34. Happy Birthday.. 63
35. Seeds of Time.. 65
36. Save the Mouse.. 66
37. The Written Word.. 68
38. Rain of Tears.. 69
39. Lake... 71
40. On Fire... 73
41. Family Circle... 74
42. Magic Chef.. 77
43. Fireworks Finale.. 79
44. Present Participles of Love... 80
45. Lost in a Dream – Part 1.. 81
46. Dream Zones – Part 2.. 82
47. Dream Need – Part 3... 83
48. A Night of Dreams – Part 4.. 84
49. Daydreaming Question – Part 5... 85
50. Dream's Wisdom – Part 6... 86
51. What I Said... 87
52. The World's Come to This.. 89
53. No Hereafter.. 90
54. Hereafter We Go Again... 91
55. Hereafter Here.. 93
56. Heavenly Hereafter.. 94
57. Palm Tree... 97
58. Winter's Deadly Beauty.. 99
59. The Double Sunshine... 100
60. Fate's Fortune.. 102
61. Sad Psyche.. 105
62. Pious Passion... 106
63. Serving King Tomorrow... 107
64. Picture Frame Life.. 109
65. Journey to Destiny.. 110
66. Weed Worthy... 113
67. Face It... 114
68. La-La Land.. 115
69. Paths... 117
70. Slippers.. 118
71. Modern Art.. 121
72. Goodbye... 122
73. Dining Room Table... 125
74. Deep.. 126
75. Tiny Bits... 129
76. I Never Met Him... 130

77. I Said So 131
78. Almost Here 133
79. Symphony Refrained 135
80. Puddle Jumping 136
81. I See You.. 137
82. State of Mine 138
83. Cliché.. 140
84. Tattooed Gardener.. 142
85. Sunset on a Florida Beach 145
86. Sixteen 147
87. Once Upon a Time 148
88. Life's Delight... 150
89. My Personal Awe's List 153
90. Magnolia Bush 157
91. Age-Old Resolution 158
92. Lady Bountiful 159
93. Fear of Fire 160
94. It's All Good 162
95. Honor.. 164
96. Hermit Crab 165
97. The Travelers 166
98. Back Seat Driver.. 168
99. This New Spring.. 171
100. Still.. 172
101. Uneasy 173
102. Congratulations... 174
103. Animal Shelter... 175
104. Play Ball... 176
105. Memories of Mom 177
106. The Western Sky.. 183
107. Pillow Talk... 184
108. Curiosity.. 186
109. Gulliver 187
110. The Wolf.. 188
111. Light the Way 189
112. Listen, Listen, Maestro Man 190
113. Blank Slate 191
114. Standing Engagement.. 193
115. An Ocean of Tears.. 195
116. Big Box... 196
117. Clean House... 197
118. Tribute to the Peony 199
119. Awakenings 200

120. Imagination's Tutor 203
121. Epitaph.. 204
Appendix 205
About the Author 219

Table of Illustrations

5. Clouds.. 6
7. Life, the Universe and Everything – Personal Perspective........................... 10
9. God's Friends.. 14
12. Wonderful Time... 22
14. The Villain.. 26
15. February Dreaming.. 28
16. Sensing Spring... 30
23. Anticipation... 45
25. Remembered Freedom... 48
28. Highway Wonder... 53
29. The Odyssey.. 54
30. Contemplating energy... 57
31. The Fulfillment of Beauty.. 59
32. Monster Within... 60
35. Seeds of Time.. 64
39. Lake... 70
41. Family Circle.. 75
42. Magic Chef... 76
43. Fireworks Finale... 78
52. The World's Come to This... 88
55. Hereafter Here... 92
57. Palm Tree.. 96
58. Winter's Deadly Beauty... 98
61. Sad Psyche.. 104
64. Picture Frame Life.. 108
66. Weed Worthy... 112
69. Paths... 116
71. Modern Art.. 120
73. Dining Room Table... 124
75. Tiny Bits... 128
78. Almost Here... 132
79. Symphony Refrained.. 134
85. Sunset on a Florida Beach... 144
86. Sixteen... 146
89. My Personal Awe's List.. 152

90. Magnolia Bush 156
99. This New Spring... 170
106. The Western Sky... 182
114. Standing Engagement... 192
118. Tribute to the Peony... 198
120. Imagination's Tutor 202

This book is dedicated to my children,
to my grandchildren,
to my descendants.
Love lives forever!

Preface

I have often wondered what my ancestors were like, both those I have known and loved, and those gone long before me. How did life treat them? What were their deepest thoughts, fears, memories? How did they perceive themselves and others?

I don't know if I am alone in this. I am just one person, a tiny speck of creation, unknown by most and probably destined to remain that way. In three or four generations, it will be as if I never existed, just as my long-ago ancestors do not exist for me today in any real way.

Maybe my children and grandchildren feel they already know me, or as much of me as they care to know. I have not made any huge difference in this world, although I have always yearned to do so. I am just ordinary, I admit – boring. But still, I wish I had something from the minds of my ordinary, boring ancestors. Therefore, I offer this to my future descendants and to any others who might care to read.

These poems are the true me: my thoughts, my observations, my opinions, my fantasies, my cares, my worries. Everything that I am is contained here, and each poem reflects something of that. I have tried to keep out religion and politics though they do peek through since I have strong thoughts and opinions on both.

I have also tried to limit nostalgia as much as possible. Yet my mind often tends to lean these days in that direction, to the past and to nature. Since I am late in starting this project, poems that I might have written in my younger days now must come from my memories of those times. My actual here and now is comprised of my family and friends, world events, gardening, my philosophical wisdom, my reading, and finally, my writing.

I have included an appendix where I attempt to explain what prompted me to write each poem. Specific lines can appear meaningless and can be hard for me to explain. Often the phrase was my best shot at putting forth my feelings and emotions, sometimes the only way, when I could not find more meaningful words.

I have done my best. I am not an accredited poet. My work probably does not fit into any official literary rules. However, these poems are who I am.

~1~
Prologue

It's about the words.
Trying to find the right ones
to entice the mind's

imagination.
I have mine and you have yours.
Let's get together

to delve times long past,
in my rhymes, my prose, my verse,
remembering how

life was lived back then.
Beauty, nature, and music,
then and now still pure.

Join me in my joys.
Share my hopes and fears and dreams,
all a part of me.

My abilities
might seem amateurish but
this feels important.

Friends and family,
you are my inspiration.
You are the reason

I have tried my best
to give you my own true self.
I am excited.

I feel privileged
to leave this piece of myself
for posterity.

JAO

October 2022

-2-

The Owl

Put it on your bed.
Put it on your desk.
Keep it in your closet.
Just look at it from time to time
and think of us,
your family and friends,
all of us who care for you.
We want to be the wise owl
in your life.
When you are alone,
when you are in class,
when you are with your friends,
wondering how to proceed,
look at the wise owl
and think of us.

J.S.D.

June 2012

~3~
The Lion

Bambi, Lion King, even Nemo.

A young Indian goes on his first hunt to test his manhood.

A young man off to college is kind of the same, I think.

Who am I? Where am I going?

All of the lessons are to be learned, the successes, the failures, in life, as well as the classroom.

Just as Lion King, Bambi and Nemo had their friends and family for support, so do you.

We are all cheering for you, applauding your triumphs, supporting you when you are distressed. You are everything to us.

Look at your Lion from time to time.

Bring him out and think of us. You are that Lion. We all exist in your Circle of Love.

J.A.O.

June 2013

~4~
Eleven Years and Fifty Days

As I turn eleven, you are born.

Jealousy and anxiety, love and pride, all live within my child's heart.

As I am confirmed, you are baptized.

Innocence and naïveté shine from both of us.

You can't remember, but we lived in Camelot then.
I think righteousness, simplicity, and love lived within everyone we knew.

As you wear white for First Communion, I am wed with whiteness perceived.

Though I am enceinte, innocence and naïveté we still both hold close.

As you are wed, I am nostalgic for my own wedding. The differences are stark. However, I find it bothers me not at all.

As your children are born, mine are leaving home.

A generation divides them.
Yet love is constant, I think.

We are both grown up now, all innocence and naïveté gone. Mine well past. Perhaps a trickle still left to you.

Now our children are grown. We become more alike, don't you think?

Eleven years and fifty days. Two different worlds. They unite then separate again. Ships crossing in the night.

J.S.D.

September 2015

Clouds – 5

~5~

Clouds

The sky is blue, bright with the sun. We are babies, fresh from our mother's womb.

When the first white fluffy cloud appears, we are delighted, our imaginations engaged.

Even though there may be some conflict as life journeys on, we can still see the fluffy clouds in the bright sunny skies. We are young. We know life will be beautiful and perfect. Perhaps we are eighteen.

Soon, the hazy mist washes away the fluff and now coats that perfect sky. Life is more difficult than we first thought, but we cope. The sun shines faintly through, and we are content.

When the first storm clouds appear, we are intrigued, drawn to the power and majesty of nature's force, insects attracted to the light of fire.

Where has the sunny puffiness gone? The dark, cloudy cold is getting old fast as also are we.

The hurricanes of hurt and loss, the tsunami of illness, the tornadoes of death are taking their toll.

Yet, just as hurricanes, tsunami and tornadoes are magnificent in their own way, as natural as the fluffy cloud in the shining blue sky, so also are hurt and loss and heartache and illness and death.

Actually, death is the return of the fluffy clouds, now backdrop to a rainbow in the shining sky, the aftermath of the storm.

JLO

September 2015

-6-

Life, the Universe and Everything
A Philosophical Perspective

Well, my friend, here we are two specks in the Universe.

Do you find the immensity and the beauty as mind-boggling as I do?

Curiosity and wonder ponder that which we cannot possibly conceive.

The Universe, bursting with constellations, solar systems, and galaxies, entices us with clues to our existence.
Yet Life must exist to complete the Universe.

This solar system is filled with planets, stars, moons, asteroids, too many to imagine.
Yet, the possibilities of Life far surpass.

Our particular planet twirls around her favorite star. She romances her devoted moon, eternally embracing her. This cosmic soap opera mimics Life as we know it.

Do we hear a tree falling in the forest? Does the Universe exist without our Life?
Have we spoken of this?

The Universe dwells within us, compelling our imagination and intellect as Life in turn dwells within the Universe.

Yet, Life's connections intrigue me more.

Simplicity and complexity define us.

Love and loyalty, tolerance and forgiveness, empathy and support, simple connections give Life meaning and purpose.

We, my friend, have made these connections with each other.
We discuss it all unending.

This is why we fit. This is our Everything.

JSD

September 2015

Life, the Universe and Everything
A Personal Perspective – 7

~7~

Life, the Universe and Everything
A Personal Perspective

The sun is shining, and Life is breathing, and we exist.

The stars twinkle. Life promises. We are friends.

The planets circle their designated stars. Life designs every path. We connect.

The moon pulls and glows while Life forgives and forgets, and we live and learn.

Meteorites are really shooting stars. Life, however, is reality. We support each other no matter how we are perceived.

Constellations map our skies as they engage our imagination. Life is a map to our past and a blueprint for our future. We care about each other, our world and everything in it.

Comets like to flash their tails as they travel through space. Life presents flashes of hope and support and generosity, tales of joy and loyalty and trust and love. We accept each other with all our flashes of wit and whimsy.

Galaxies burst forth into being while Life is actually being alive. We talk about all this and more.

The Universe exists and nurtures. Life begins and lives and dies and completes the Universe. We have stood the test of time.

Everything is as it should be.

September 2015

~8~

Tinkle Bell

You came to us in our darkest year,
Tinkle Bell sprinkling her fairy dust, vanquishing every fear.
Into our dreams you sparked a tiny light to our future hope.
With this beginning, we now can cope.

How bout that tiny baby keeping us too busy to despair? Mom's
always watching over her despite having so much to bear.

We watched you grow with love and truth.
We all rejoiced in your deep youth.

How bout that baby-child striving to grow strong and fit? Mom is
keeping her snug and safe always working to manage it.

Our tomboy evolves as her childhood flowed.
Animals and gymnastics, her passions explode.

But

puberty brings rebellion. The strings are hard to cut.
Teen years are complex. Everyone thinks they know what's what.
Recognition is difficult to achieve. To fantasy you wish to cleave.

How bout our woman-child? She's breaking free, flying wild. But
Mom's confused, both mean and mild.

Coming of age is all achieved?
Graduation, marriage, motherhood, how can you be so peeved?

Education enriches your mind, and that is fine.
Marriage brings happiness, at least for a time.
Motherhood is about it all.
Doubt and worry and love in thrall.

How bout our new grownup girl? She faces life with courage and pride, taking it all in her stride. Mom's still striving for control, unwilling to let her baby go.

Life is full of love and joy.
She knows the risks are not a ploy.
Optimism is the rule. She cannot fail.
She's no one's fool.
Life could never be so cruel.

How bout our baby, our girl? Although her mom has now been stilled, she makes us all feel so thrilled, our tiny light and hope fulfilled.

J.A.Q.

February 2016

God's Friends – 9

~9~

God's Friends

God said to His friends, "It's again that time to make another one of Mine.
You I leave to greet, to give, to guide this one through thick and thin until it's all been done."

So my existence came to be, that time in space when God made me.
This is how my life moved through when God's friends arrived with work to do.

Childhood came and went too fast. It's just a blur. I'm very sure it was a blast.
Now it's in the past because it simply could not last.

But in that time His friends did shine.

A tireless turtle, greenish blue, labored long to amuse me when I was two.
With the social squirrel and funny bunny, we played all day until exhaustion had its say.
A funky fish when I was five, I watched him as he did his dive.

As time goes by, I need to fly, or maybe soar, just plain old roar.
My imagination at the fair watching horses can take me there.

From the hummingbird to the eagle, the robin and sea gull, so wild, so wondrous they make me smile.
They certainly know how to beguile!
I hear them squeak. I hear them squawk. I see them all avoid the hawk.

And then I know that just like them I can live and love and win!

As twilight will now approach, no longer does my life reproach.
Kit and Pup have been my friends.
My cat and dog, my soul they cleanse.
They purr and bark and nudge and nag.
They don't allow my life to lag.

They're always there. They never hate. They teach forgiveness is not too late.

When I am anxious, sad, or bored, they are there. They're my reward. My spirit is lifted. There is no question. My mood has shifted.

They give so much. My heart they touch.

Sad to say they always leave. Thus, they teach me how to grieve.

When my time comes as come it must, God's friends will have fulfilled His trust.

J.A.D.

February 2016

~10~

Party Time

Eat, drink and be merry.
It's party time, so let's not tarry!

Our daily bread
a worthy spread
with meat and potatoes.
Don't forget the tomatoes!

A pinch of salt as easy as pie,
the pizza and wings are in a tie.

A piece of cake with no spilled milk,
we must eat and drink while chilled.

We have our cake and eat it too
but the cookies crumble. That's nothing new.

Apple, peaches, pumpkin pie,
we want to eat them. That's no lie.

An apple a day
keeps the doctor away
but sour grapes will make us pay.

Spill the beans and bring home the bacon.
It's party time and all is taken.

Two peas in a pod in our salad days,
be a good egg and mend your ways.

Use your noodle and do not doodle.
We must take time to eat some strudel.

Cool as a cucumber and brown as a berry.
Down the hatch goes a refreshing sherry.

On the wagon and one for the road,
it tastes so good. Please do not scold.

The proof is in the pudding.
It's party time! Do not be brooding!

J.S.C.

September 2015

~11~

Sonnet to the Clouds

Fluffy, white clouds dot the shining blue sky.
How enchanted we are as wide-eyed youth.
We know life will be splendid when we try.
Nothing can go wrong and that is the truth.

Hazy mist now coats that shining blue sky.
The sun still shows through, and we are content.
Life will have trials which cause us to sigh
though we can deal with them as they present.

But large, dark clouds bring the frightening storms
like hurt and heartache and illness and death.
We all have grown old as the sorrow forms.
It is now difficult to take a breath.

Death is the storm with a true aftermath.
A rainbow gives hope we're on the right path.

JSD

February 2016

Wonderful Time – 12

~12~
Wonderful Time

Come dance with me
whispered the wind chimes to the wind.
Let's waltz together and let me feel
your breezy breath upon me.
Let's rock the ages
to the rhythm of your growing excitement.
Let's dance for joy
and whirl and twirl and twist and tangle and have a wonderful time.

Come sing to me
begged the moon of the earth wolf.
Lament the lullabies of days long gone.
Bark and bay your sweet ballads
of love and life as I pull you
into my shimmering embrace.
Howl hymns of happiness and praise and God,
simple songs that serve us well.
Let's sing for joy because life is a wonderful time.

Come play with me
pled the puppy to his siblings.
Wriggle and roll with me
in the sandbox of our youth.
Grunt and growl and wrestle with me.
Tug my tail and spin me round and round and
run with me until we are all done.
We always play together in joyful abandon
and we have a wonderful time.

Come laugh with me
called the clown to the crowd.
Laugh at all my jokes and
pranks and puns of wit and whimsy.
Laugh wrinkles are the best kind,
and laughter is the best medicine
as fun never hurt anyone,

or so I have been told.
Appreciate my antics and my wisecracks,
winking and wincing all the way.
Laughing for joy is a wonderful time.

Come cry with me
my country's law urged its land.
Weep with me when we are weary
with worry, aching
to bring back times long past.
Wail with me about life's injustices. We must
work together to do what must be done.
Now let the tears wash away all fears as we wait
in joyful anticipation for
the return of the wonderful times.

Come be with me
every person asks the other.
Let's dance and sing and play and laugh and cry.
Let's share our joy because
together we will make a wonderful time.

JAD

February 2016

~13~
Pain's Prayer

Take Your Hand and
Wipe It Away.
God.
Pain.
So Selfish!
Oh God!
All Pain.
(But please do mine first.)

J.A.O.

2/17/2016

The Villain – 14

~14~

The Villain

Anxiety is a villain so tough
he invades every facet of the mind.
Without mercy, he will make our life rough
unless there is an answer we can find.

Our villain has a mate called depression.
She's a fiend, who with her lover will lurk
within those souls who suffer repression.
That darkness is where they do their best work.

They have two offspring named fear and worry.
Together they make a frightening crew.
They deal out despair we try to bury
by hiding our heartache and making do.

This family we really need to fight
by working together to find the light.

JLO

February 2016

February Dreaming – 15

~15~
February Dreaming

It's springtime in the garden of my dreams.
The cold earth has thawed and now becomes kind
to earth's fertility where sunshine beams
after plow and plant of my springtime mind.
It's February. My mind knows no bound.
My youth and spring garden are briefly found.

Spring toil's rewards in my mid-summer's head
are plump rose buds and my supple new form.
Sweet peas and lilies are a perfumed bed.
Here daydreams and daisies together warm
hearts living in this February cold.
They provide gladness and pleasures untold.

My garden yields bounty in autumn's time
and my body is at its youthful peak.
Cornstalks and pumpkins are now in their prime
and muscles strengthen each day of the week.
Days are now short. My dream begins once more.
It's springtime again which makes my heart soar.

Reality gives a jolt to my dreams.
It's February and my body aches.
Time wears down gardens and people. It seems
one will come back but the other forsakes.
February is my fantasy time,
dreaming of gardens where all is sublime.

JLO

February 2016

Sensing Spring – 16

~16~

Sensing Spring

I know it's coming for sure,
that special scent, clean and pure.
The soil holds a pungent smell.
Can't resist. I know this well.
Who can forget the flowers?
Inhale and sniff their powers!
Rain and soil and air will bring
something that means I smell spring.

Raindrops landing on my tongue
taste like nectar, every one.
The early foods that we can grow
make my taste buds really flow.
Truly what I hunger for:
warmth and daylight more and more.
In varied ways we can wring
those terrific tastes of spring.

So many things we can touch.
To list them all is too much.
The rain as it hits my face.
Sunshine's warmth when it's in place.
Push your hands through fertile earth
and you know this season's worth.
I love the breeze's early sting.
It's safe to say I feel spring.

Vibrations within my ear
tell me that the season's near.
Thunder growls, and we prepare.
Raindrops splatter everywhere.
Springtime ears let us enjoy
the rustling dance trees employ.
We can't forget birds that sing.
It's everywhere I hear spring.

Eyes will reflect springtime's soul
as we watch the season grow.
Diamond raindrops drip from trees.
A drenched earth is now so pleased.
Newborn green has pushed on through.
Soon flowers will blossom too!
Baby leaves to branches cling.
Now I'm sure that I see spring.

Winter's deep and long and cold.
My senses still are untold.
It's a while before they know
that sap has begun to flow.
But still when it's in the air,
although the trees are still bare,
winter has had its last fling.
This I know when I smell spring!

JLD

March 2016

~17~
Longing for Spring

It's here at last!
It has begun.
Warm rains.
Damp earth.
Sweet scents and sunny skies.
Newborn grass.
Fuzzy baby leaves.
Pussy willows, flowers, and baby birds.
Here today.
Tomorrow gone.
But forever
rooted in memory.

JLO

March 2016

~18~
Rejuvenation

Heed this advice and be reborn.
Prepare to enter a sacred sanctuary
by shedding your cares and worries
along with your clothing
into the dirty laundry pile.
Prepare mind and body for a special experience
as sweet hot bubbles await.

Now in this delightful domain
stretch your body and take a deep breath.
Pour the golden elixir under the opened faucet of heat and watch
as future pleasure fills the tub like finest champagne into a crystal
goblet.
Sense what is coming. Listen to the rush of water like sunbeam-
splattered
waterfalls splashing into the river below, exploding into foam-filled
waves.
Sink into a world of pure bliss and feel your body's relief.
Inhale the exhilarating scent as you sigh in contentment.
Sweet hot bubbles pop in joyous anticipation.

Now lay your head upon some cushioning towels
and settle back into sudsy serenity.
Meditate and let your consciousness be soothed.
Enjoy the purity of total tranquility
as the holiness of it all fills you with subliminal energy.
Sweet hot bubbles caress your body.

Lie there forever. Admire your wrinkled fingertips.
Let them wander over the wondrous perfumed silkiness
that is your skin.
Relax and close your eyes and dream.
Feel the renewal of your soul as
sweet hot bubbles surround you.

Sweet hot bubbles are disappearing!
Scrub away the stubborn remnants of anger and fear
and your skin will glow.
Shampoo and rinse your hair, squeezing out all sadness.
Be ready now to step back into life, refreshed and pristine because
sweet hot bubbles have worked their magic.

Acknowledge the time has come to pull the plug, letting it all go
down the drain
along with the water.
Brisk application of towel and brush invigorates body, mind, and
soul.
The world awaits your re-entrance. You need to catch up with your
laundry.

J.A.O.

March 2016

~19~

Sequel to The Owl

It's a day for celebration!
An owlet is born today.
We have been his owl role model,
collective wisdom that doesn't prey.
But now he's on his way! See him spread his wings!
His flight begins!

A metamorphosis has begun today.
Spin your head round and open your eyes wide.
An owl can't stay an owl but will turn into prey
unless he follows the owl's way.
Experience of people, places, and things,
good judgment, hard work, and smart choices
are the wise owl's true prey.

This is the day all begins anew.
Learn as much as you can and then some.
It takes a long time for an owlet to fledge,
and each feather fledged carries a truth
to be savored, a step in your life's journey.
You will have arrived
when you realize your destination is to be
that owlet with gray hair
perching on the ledge
of knowledge and wisdom.

This is the sequel I didn't think about yesterday.
But now I know the sequels will keep coming
because you have become The Owl.

JS.D

May 2016

~20~
My Decades Journal

In the forties, this boomer arrived,
child of the "Greatest Generation."
I was one of many who survived
to become the bulk of our nation.
The forties gave me only a year.
Not much from that time is very clear.

I always knew that all moms stayed home,
and in that home there lived a father.
From that story we should never roam.
To do so would be such a bother.
Fifties were where I lived my childhood.
I was lucky. Mine was very good.

The sixties were full of discontent,
such as Vietnam and civil rights.
I was not sure what all of this meant.
I just knew there were plenty of fights.
The sixties were when I came of age.
It was time to leave my childhood cage.

Seventies saw feminism grow.
I had not yet learned to be concerned.
It was not a time for status quo.
It was necessary that I learned.
This decade made me a young adult.
I finally joined that grownup cult.

Eighties were my time to fix my past,
to make changes while I was still young.
The differences to me were vast,
though others thought they were too far-flung.
In this decade there was lots of time.
After all, I was still in my prime.

We saw the world change beyond belief.
Computers and cell phones exploded.
Some jobs were lost, causing us great grief,
but good jobs were never outmoded.
In the nineties I started to think
that the world was beginning to shrink.

Few live through a new millennium.
Fear and frenzy thrived as you might guess.
But troubles were at a minimum
though Y2K caused a lot of stress.
The aughts were well named I must agree,
contemplating where I ought to be.

It's awkward to talk about the tens.
I certainly am no longer young.
It doesn't matter. They are my lens
to the future and how it is sprung.
I am living in the tens right now.
Decades left will be the best I vow.

JAO

April 2016

~21~
Tis the Season

Just as the sun rises and sets,
just as the moon waxes and wanes,
the bills must be paid each month.
From utilities to mortgage to credit cards,
to ensure that life goes on,
the bills must be paid each month.

Just as the earth revolves around the sun
tax season arrives each year.
Just as the world would end if the sun rebuffed the earth,
to ignore the tax man would be at your peril.
So, each year we file with the Internal Revenue Service,
then carefully pack the previous year away
into a blue, plastic storage bin.
The attic is now bursting with fifty storage bins
each jam-packed with a year's tale of earning, spending, and saving.

Our finances are tucked away in blue storage bins
ready to be mined at a moment's notice.
Would that my mind's data be so readily available!
So many sweet memories, sparkling like diamonds,
are buried within its deep, dark caverns.
A pickaxe would be handy for chiseling out each precious jewel
year by year. Like my blue storage bins,
how satisfying it would be if I could dislodge a year, say 1977,
and browse each day of living, loving, and learning.

Fifty blue storage bins need to be whittled down so that the attic
might breathe.
I start with the 1977 container to see what might be discarded.
Income tax forms, National Grid, and other bills abound.
But I find my tuition statement for attending Syracuse University.
Birthday cards congratulate me on turning twenty-eight.
I see the Christmas we gave our four-year-old daughter and nine-
year-old son.
I bought my first car that year, a 1978 Honda Civic wagon.

We moved to our new home on Parsons Drive.
All are hard-copy gems of living, loving, and learning.

These gems have pick-axed my mind and freed precious memories.
In them, I see my children grow and thrive.
I see our lives improving.
I see the many paths we could have chosen, and those we did.
I now understand how my country's investments
have paved some of these paths.
Tis the season to pay the tax man, invest in a new blue storage bin
and pack away another memorable year
of living, loving, and learning.

May 2016

~22~

Sweet Home

The bowels were wrapped in poison.
The old top hat, frayed and drooping
could no longer protect the body.
The skin was aged, damaged by the sun,
and the body needed a bath.
The arteries and veins were blocked
while the heart sported a band-aid.
This body had lost its head
so there was no one to make decisions.
The body mourned the loss of its head.

A new head must be found, or the body will die.
A new head would consult the physician, the surgeon,
who would remove the poison,
thus healing the bowels.
Facelift and skin graft bring back a youthful glow to the body
and a good bath would make all the difference.
Rip off the band-aid and prepare for transplant.
Bypass the bad arteries and stent the veins.
Also, a sheltering new top hat should be secured.
The body is resuscitated

for it has found
a new head that also mourns.
One that agrees to the attachment
because it recognizes the dignity and value
hidden within the body,
one that appreciates home.
This body has found its way back.
It knows that individual heads come and go.
But as long as the body can hold a loving head
life goes on.

JAD

May 2016

~23~
Anticipation

It's too hot today!
All plant life crisps.
Animals stifle in their coats
except insects.
They are busy gorging on party punch blood.
In this desert we are parched.
In this sauna we sweat.
The sidewalks steam.
The cruel sun is merciless.

It's too cold today!
A new ice age has dawned.
Life on this stark tundra is a bleak place
where frozen gray statues pretend to live.
The numbness sinks in
and bones creak.
Plants and animals and humans hibernate
seeking precious relief and refuge.
The sun keeps its distance, withholding its comforting warmth.

It's so nice out today!
Finally! Just perfect!
Balmy breezes conspire with the soothing sun.
It's a day for plants and animals and people to play.
It's a day when work feels like vacation.
It seems the world is smiling, celebrating
the return of a yearned-for event.
The never-ending labor pains of yesterday are forgotten as
this long-awaited child is born.

JSD

May 2016

Anticipation – 23

~24~
Old Fashioned Summer

When kids start shouting that school's out
it's time for fun without a doubt.

Roller skates and hopscotch to begin,
then jump rope and hula hoops that spin.
We bike to the park for crafts and swings.
A Boondoggle gift for family brings
oohs and aahs and praise all around.
Now bike back to the pool, swimming bound.

From dawn til dusk, we play most days.
Running races, tag, and ball are some ways.
"Apple, peaches, pumpkin pie" shout some
or "Ready or not here I come!"
Red Light, Red Rover, and Duck, Duck Goose,
and Hide and Seek all set us loose.

We play badminton and tennis when we have a net
or fly kites in the park at sunset.
Mostly imagination rules the days.
We have makeshift tents and made-up plays.
We are kings and queens and even horses.
Unlimited are our sources.

We run through sprinklers, rain, and puddles.
Flowers we pick and trade for cuddles.
Peanut butter or baloney for lunch
and on hot days we love to crunch
a Fudgsicle or Popsicle,
our five-cent summer's icicle.

Lightning bugs we spot in twilight
to catch in jars is a highlight.
After dark when the world is eerie
we tell stories to make us leery.
On special nights our neighbors might see
us run the street and scream with glee.

On holidays like July Fourth
we wave our sparklers back and forth.
When the weather's so bad it rains
there are cards and games and dolls and trains.
Never does a day go by
without something to occupy.

Finally, it's time for State Fair fun.
Now we know summer's over. It's done!

J.A.O.

June 2016

Remembered Freedom – 25

-25-
Remembered Freedom

Anticipation is high
in these first days of June.
We remember the revelry
and revere
the energy and life lust
whirling in the air,
with summer's dog days as distant
as destiny.
Birds are in their summer homes
living the good life.
The sun sparkles above
the beckoning water
and we are hypnotized by the sweet scent
of long forgotten freedom.

J.L.C.

June 2016

~26~
For Alex

You're a sixth-grade grad so this is for you.
It's now time to share what I know is true.
Happiness in life is the perfect goal
with love and contentment deep in your soul.

It's important to find what you enjoy.
The trick is to build and not to destroy.
Friends, pets, gaming, baseball or whatever,
any might be your future endeavor.

I know school often seems boring and strict.
Keep your eyes on your goals and I predict
you can do it. You are so very smart.
You just need to think and follow your heart.

I know you want for your life to move on
but that future life will be built upon
the choices you make in the next few years.
Studying today brings tomorrow's cheers.

June 2016

-27-
Truth Denied

What is our country but a promise?
Begging for fulfillment from its citizens,
trusting in our collective wisdom
to preserve the beauty revered by all,
to protect its people one and all,
to thrive.
Who can tell lie from truth?
Collectively we decide,
each hoping for their chosen truth.

Faith is the belief in a promise.
Hope is trust that the promise is not a lie.
Love is acceptance of the promise,
the truth and the lie.
Truth does not need faith, hope or love
because it is true.
Hope that the promise is true,
making it easy to love and accept.
Otherwise, it must be a lie
and not worthy of faith, hope, or love.
Sometimes lies are truth denied.

What does it mean to love one's country
but to have faith and hope in its promise?
One man's truth is another man's lie.
But our country is still a promise
true to someone.

J.A.O.

June 2016

~28~
Highway Wonder

In my time there was a meadow
filled with light and fantasy. A place where
faeries formed diamonds from raindrops
and painted wildflowers with rainbow remnants.
Elves dipped into the pots of gold found beneath,
diligently gleaming each blade of grass.

Too soon a dirt road appeared
pressed down by those resolved
to witness the grandeur of light and fantasy.
Like shooting stars and aurora borealis,
a natural wonder
cherished by all.

Eventually a little store
surrounded by a parking lot was built,
needed to satisfy souvenir cravings.
The meadow shrunk just a bit,
its glowing glory dimmed by cheap tokens
of light and fantasy.

Soon the store became rickety
and it was torn down
for the new highway
paved with good intentions,
snuffing out the light
and burying fantasy.

Everyone is excited,
trying to reach
that precious paradise of old,
trying to recapture the wonder
of light and fantasy
now gone forever.

JLD

June 2016

Highway Wonder – 28

The Odyssey – 29

~29~

The Odyssey

Look at that couple starting their walk.
It's that time of day for them to talk.
There's always so much they can discuss.
Not much misses their collective eye.
When they see changes, they question why
their opinions are superfluous.

Look at that couple now walking by.
They don't want to stumble so they try
avoiding broken sidewalks and curbs,
leery of cars, kids, and unleashed dogs.
All are reviewed in their dialogues.
Still, they trod on so nothing disturbs.

Look at that couple keep walking on.
It really is a phenomenon.
Each friendly stranger becomes a friend.
Every cat or dog is their own
to reassure with a calming tone.
A nod and smile they always extend.

Look at that couple walking today.
They find pleasure viewing nature's way.
They watch ducks in the burbling brook
and savor scents of newly mown grass.
Birdsong always stops them as they pass.
They stand a while to listen and look.

Look at that couple walking along.
They started out determined and strong.
They conquered obstacles big and small,
approaching home revived and relieved.
Still, they're weary and glad they're reprieved.
Tomorrow's a new day they recall.

JLO

June 2016

~30~
Contemplating Energy

I'm trying to get up the energy
to move, to do something,
to make a difference somehow.

But here I sit
in this easy chair
staring into space
contemplating my oughts.

Dishes pile and dust defiles.
My vacuum sulks while
my office wants work today
and my garden won't go away.

My oughts overwhelm.
The best I seem to be able to do is read,
or look at my phone.
This makes me feel tired and alone.

I want to write, to create,
but I cannot.
I want to call my children,
chat with my neighbors,
visit my friends,
go shopping.
Anything.

I need to move, to do something,
to make a difference.
But here I sit,
contemplating.

JSD

July 2016

Contemplating Energy – 30

~31~
The Fulfillment of Beauty

Every garden needs a birdbath
with a fountain that bubbles or spritzes,
and mine is no exception.
I imagine the soothing sounds as the tiny waterfall
tinkles into the bowl, shimmering outward,
refracting sunny rays into rippling waves.
Hummingbirds take delicate sips as they flit above
and bluebirds and goldfinches dance,
playing water games together in their stone pool.
Bright butterflies flutter about
in my mind's serendipitous scene.

After a while
my garden acquired a bubbling birdbath
and finally, some birds arrived.
It seems my birdbath has become an exclusive spa
claimed by the crow, the blackbird, and the pigeon.
I watch them roll and bounce in raucous enjoyment,
emptying the bowl as they bathe and blunder about
shedding their filthy remnants
of feathers, feces, and dirt.
Wasps happily buzz above the fountain
and frolic in its mucky residue.

This is a different serendipity
that feeds my soul's satisfaction.
I sometimes ponder the meaning
of perceived beauty and realistic beauty,
how one is adored and the other ignored.
My garden needed a birdbath
so that its beauty could be lifted to a place
where usefulness meets need,
invitations extend to all,
and beauty has meaning.

J.S.D.

July 2016

The Fulfillment of Beauty – 31

Monster Within – 32

~32~
Monster Within

Monsters hiding under the bed, in the closet
are real.
Alone in the evening,
in the deepest, darkest hours
we know this.

The monster haunts
soul and spirit, our very being,
with recognition of itself
in our mind's mirror.

Demons delve deep
into the abyss of the psyche
and we do dance with them.
Horror is always hungry,
ready to devour.

From innocent youth to wizened elders,
no one is immune to the waking nightmare.
Supernatural, alien creatures
dwell deep, seemingly invincible
since they are part of us.

The monster within is the message.
We are truly alone in our aloneness
as we were in the womb
and will be in the grave,
as we stand before the universe.

July 2016

~33~
Changing of the Guard

Two old cars considered their crash.
They wish they could have rearranged
circumstances that would have changed
the end of their drivers' mad dash.

Though these two were from the old school
they knew they lacked safety features.
But they were proud to be teachers
to their heirs, the current carpool.

They taught them to work hard and stay
committed to reaching their goals,
focused on what the future knows
will surely be coming their way.

A new world with cars we don't drive,
born without steering wheel or brakes.
It's a brand-new design which makes
it easier to stay alive.

Drunk driving, texting, and road rage,
those things and more their drivers do
would no longer matter. They knew
statistics would be a good gauge.

Travel would be forever changed,
giving new life to those grown old.
No more teen tragedies to hold
their parents forever deranged.

Two old cars towed to a junk yard
feel sadness for their people's pain.
They know the world will be more sane
when comes the changing of the guard.

August 2016

~34~
Happy Birthday

It's my birthday today
and I would like to say
I'm glad to still be here
to celebrate this year
with candles on my cake.

Yet now I need to make
sure my conscience is clear
because I hold too dear
the value of money
and a life that's sunny.

Render me gifts and song
but make sure I belong
to a world that survived,
where no one is deprived
of basic daily needs
caused by my selfish deeds.

Though I work very hard
always trying to guard
my rights to everything
I expect life to bring,

I forgot about you,
the lot in life you drew,
forgot it could be me
trying to make my plea
to a world so cruel.
It's obvious that you'll
not have happy birthdays
but try to hold back tears
and struggle through the years
without a voice to raise.

August 2016

Seeds of Time – 35

~35~
Seeds of Time

Methuselah, a five-thousand-year-old
pine in California
has stood through the ages.
Hidden, lest man destroy
Father Time himself.

Gazing at trees is like
looking into a reverse crystal ball,
one that sees into the past,
one that recognizes its ancestors.
When they planted trees
our forefathers planted our past's future.
If they but knew
or perhaps they do.

Observe the maple seedling, the acorn, the pinecone
littering the land,
a glimpse into nature's nursery.
Know that to cultivate tomorrow's trees
is to console Methuselah.
In each tree's survival
time itself survives,

evolving into a new world
where we live on
in a crystal ball,
giving homage to Methuselah now found,
witnessing newborn seedlings,
our future's future.

JAD

August 2016

~36~
Save the Mouse

Consider the dog
enjoying home-baked treats
and a personalized bed where he snoozes
contentedly.
Or the cat
luxuriating in cozy cosseted comfort,
stalking her sophisticated toys.
Rejoice in their sweet innocence,
these adored fur babies in their forever homes.

Retire the old racehorses.
Let them live out their old age
grazing the grasslands.
Allow the cows and pigs and chicks
to live life "as nature intended."
Pity the mouse,
the indignities suffered
in the name of research.

Please remember
to raise the dog, the cat, the horse,
as well as farmyard friends
with compassionate care and love.
Remember to acknowledge
that they also have feelings,
suffer pain.
Please, save the mouse!

Try to forget
there is no refuge for the refugee,
no home for the homeless,
no food for the hungry.
The sick are left to die.

They deserve everything they get
and they get what they deserve.
Every man is an island,

no second chance, no hand-up, no hope,
just indignities suffered
in the name of indifference.

J.A.O.

August 2016

~37~

The Written Word

Writers dream
to publish,
to see their narratives
nestled between hard covers
kept in libraries
for posterity.

Editors wonder
whether their work is really real
if not viewed
at newspaper stands,
smelling of fresh paper print ink
that leaves its mark upon each reader.

Historians ponder
Gutenberg's reaction to
the extinction of the printing press.
Would he be aghast,
or would he rejoice
in a new revolution?

I wonder
will the world bemoan
its future library,
a computer café?
The written word
residing in the clouds.

JSD

September 2016

~38~
Rain of Tears

Eyes cannot shed tears
in this land of depressing desiccation
where flames of heat scorch
the withered land.
Life thirsts.
The sky has forgotten how to cry.

When comes the flooding,
gates are forced open by
vengeful waves of devastation.
The rivers bloat
with unending tears of sorrow
that don't know how to stop.

Ah, but the tears of joy
as rain rolls down
the face of the earth,
greening the landscapes,
imbuing relief and hope.
Tears that promise
new beginnings and second chances.

JLO

September 2016

Lake – 39

~39~

Lake

Water, that pure gift of fluid life
will sometimes sit in an ice carved bowl
of beauty. When gifted to our sight
magnificence and majesty glow.
Everyone's invited to partake
in the serenity of the lake.

Sometimes storms are seen in the distance.
Low rumbles and a faraway flash
give hints to the coming existence
of whipping winds and huge waves that crash.
A relentless rush across the lake
will wallop the shores before they break.

Sailboats glide on the shimmering blue.
Balmy breezes catch an angel's wing.
They raced with the seagulls as they flew
like Icarus. To the sun they fling
themselves, hoping not to melt or break,
hoping for salvation from the lake.

In sweltering heat there's much to do.
Relaxation on a sunbaked beach,
diving and swimming to name a few
ways of refreshment that are in reach.
Though there are sharp shells, maybe a snake,
everyone gravitates toward the lake.

When tree leaves are flaming gold and red,
when beauty's bowl is calm and serene,
nature bids Narcissus from the dead
to witness what surpasses his mien,
to die again from a jealous ache.
There's a new reflection on the lake.

When Jack Frost brings his coldest weather,
on a diamond surface all can skate,

or fisherman with skin like leather
can saw rounded holes and cast their bait.
Though all seems lifeless on a cold lake
if you look hard, you'll see life awake.

It's so beautiful it's crystal clear,
a source of joy to be handed down
to our children so they can be near
this true jewel in creation's crown.
There's so much pleasure we all should take
from this pure gift of water, this lake.

JS·D

September 2016

~40~
On Fire

You are on the brink.
Your torch blazes,
lit with dreams,
kindled by education,
burning to change the world.

Tongues of discourse and decency
flame forth,
igniting new ideas
as flames of excitement
pursue the possibilities.

Your heart is an inferno,
exploding with sparks of integrity,
in recognition of reason
that desires to distinguish
fact from fallacy.

The dove fans the flame
even as it soothes.
Peace and love dwell
in the smoldering ashes.

JLO

September 2016

~41~
Family Circle

Electrons circle my nucleus
bound to me
by magnetic personalities,
positive of belonging
to each other
despite the negatives.

My friends and family
are planets
circling my sun.
I radiate love and trust,
turning each of them
into suns for me to circle.

My dearly departed
still circle me.
I feel them
as their energy
penetrates my memory.
I can't let them go
as I spin round and round.

We are all electrons
bound to the nucleus of eternity
and the supreme sun.
We continue to circle
each other
in an Olympic emblem of love.

JAD

September 2016

Family Circle – 41

Magic Chef – 42

~42~
Magic Chef

Chop, slice, dice, marinate.
Bake, broil, or boil
the five food groups
on that perfect pyramid
that sustains us.

Eat, devour, gobble down
every goodness in life
prepared by the magic chef
of culinary delight
residing in a capable kitchen.

Sad souls lacking the magic,
those dismal diners of distress
must eat to live.
Their GE cooker
knows no tricks.

But there are places
where magic is made each day.
Here one might live to eat
fabulous food
at a mellow meal.

Here is a new home,
in a nest
of filling possibilities
where our nurturing nature
reclaims its neediness.

Who will bring food
to the opened beaks
of these baby birds?
It is our host that lovingly stuffs
the gullets of starving cowbirds.

October 2016

Firework's Finale – 43

~43~
Fireworks Finale

Fall is the culmination,
the affirmation
of spring's fulfilled promises,
of summer's existence.
Nature's own fireworks display,
magnificent beyond all other,
bursts into glorious color,
loud and life-affirming,
the autumnal finale.

Fall gives thanks
in a seasonal celebration
of life's fullness.
Allow the showering sparkles
to dazzle and delight
before they finally fizzle
into the night,
before fall fades into
winter's waiting darkness.

October 2016

~44~
Present Participles of Love

Simply *living* together is a feat
of *giving* yourselves every day of the week.
Trusting your union to persevere
means *sharing* each other's triumphs and tears.

Working together and apart is routine
and *playing* provides the balance you need.
Still, you both are *growing*,
ceaselessly *seeking* your dreams,
thereby *learning* whatever life means.

Achieving goals that are in reach
begins with *discussing* details.
You know that *compromising* contains
the potential for *planning*,
where *agreeing* is all that remains.

Grieving though heartbreaking,
when done with *praying*
will pull you through.
Soothing each other can be a balm
for the *changing* needed before the calm.

Modeling the treatment you would like to receive
means *embracing* each other's endeavors,
always *defending* against attack,
always *protecting* each other's back.
Mainly it comes down to just *being there*
always *loving*, always sincere.

Lastly, there is *remembering*, so I present
twenty-five participles for twenty-five years of love,
now and forever your covenant.

JLD

October 2016

-45-
Lost in a Dream – Part 1

Once in a dream I was lost
in a land that I should know.
I keep wandering past sights
as clear to me as myself.
I have often traveled this road.
I recognize myself on the path.
Yet where I am I do not know.
Endlessly trekking the streets,
searching for who knows what.
Desperately recognizing
what I am looking for
is somewhere nearby,
as close as a dream.

December 2016

~46~
Dream Zones – Part 2

Remember the dream
before it flies away
on wings of dust.
Just a moment ago
I was in another dimension
living and loving life.

Where has it gone?
I need to recall.
So sure I am
that it is necessary
to remember
what is important
before it is too late.

Re-enter the dream
if that is even a possibility.
One must give up being
to achieve such a feat,
gliding from one realm
to the next and back again.

JAD.

December 2016

~47~
Dream Need – Part 3

Once upon a dream
I needed to scream
but I didn't know how
so I thought I'd allow
myself to calm down,
to take a look around.

I'm no longer earth bound
and I notice no sound.
I know not where I am.
I know not who I am.
But I know that I am
the one in a dream,
the one needing to scream.

Though it's only a dream
it might be extreme
if I asked myself why
I want to cry.
Do I think I will die
if I cannot redeem
myself in a dream?

J.A.O.

December 2016

~48~
A Night of Dreams – Part 4

I sat with my second-grade class
in a church
because we needed to pray.
Piously I considered
each face so distinct and dear,
and they stare back and shun me.

There were woven baskets all about
containing the stars of the sea,
salted by oceans, and moss
wrapping the tiny babe
of my body
that was me.

As I ran from the sea,
I entered the house
that was home,
but I'd never seen it before
even though I am sure
I have always lived there.

The electric was off
so I plugged it into
a whirlpool of current
twirling me to its center,
draining me to the oblivion
of wakefulness.

J.S.D.

December 2016

-49-
Daydreaming Question – Part 5

Who daydreams?
Perhaps the infant
staring at a world
of color and cold
and blinding brightness.
She dreams of her past
life in the womb
as the world pulls her forth
into forgetfulness.

Who daydreams?
An inattentive child in
his classroom of confusion.
For what does he yearn
other than the comfort of young childhood
and the warmth of his mother's arms?
He struggles against the world
as it pulls him forth
into conformity.

Who daydreams
in that long expanse called adulthood?
I can't speak for others, of course,
since they are not me.
Glitter and greed,
Learning and love,
Safety and salvation
before the world pulls us forth
into death.

Who daydreams
but that ghost of ourselves
escaping reality
to live in the future
or perhaps the past.

December 2016

~50~
Dream's Wisdom – Part 6

There's a time of day we all go to sleep.
It doesn't matter if you're rich or poor.
Another place awaits where some will weep.
But for others it's where they now can soar.

There's a quality in this land like life.
Though vague and turned inside out, it still seems
that good and evil even there are rife,
but choice and control disappear in dreams.

Though this strange world can be a source of joy
to try to grasp and hold in memory,
there can also be nightmares that destroy
the very last drop of serenity.

But colorful or stark, dreams don't foretell
if a world awake be heaven or hell.

December 2016

~51~

What I Said

I always knew
how they could cut,
leaving one feeling
sick to the pit
of a weeping, bleeding heart.

Pain explodes
and the hurt haunts
an upset stomach
full of guilt.
The body aches
from the wound of regret

that even time will not heal.
Too late I learned
that words can never
be taken back
into the mucky, mean mouth
that uttered the ugliness.

J.A.O.

December 2016

The World's Come to This – 52

~52~

The World's Come to This

On a gray winter's day
there lived the world vulnerable
to the menace of men,
the whims of women,
since both do revel
in the holiness of their god worship.

Somewhere are the stars
in the sea of the sky
and the sky of the sea
where lives all hope
that sparkles or shines
in a longing loneliness for change.

The wind wraps its cloak
hiding within itself
howling at humanity,
hoping to whirl its wrathful grief
but finally delving deep
into earth's comfort.

What's a world to do
but cry for mercy?
Maudlin it might seem
watching hope struggle
where god battles god
and the world weeps.

JLO

December 2016

-53-
No Hereafter

If there is no hereafter,
someday we will no longer exist,
which begs the question
whether we ever did.

Existence exists
only for the living
who ultimately die
into non-existence.

At some point each person
did not exist until they did.
Some say they lived
but then they didn't.

Some say we frantically live
in order to rest in peace,
but resting requires existence,
and peace is a condition for the living.

When the world finally dies,
the nothingness will probably question
if ever there lived a world,
if ever there was such a thing as time,
such a thing as a beginning or an end.

Now there is no one to verify
the exuberating excitement
that existed in a vast universe
of light and dark.
All is gone if it ever was.

January 2017

~54~
Hereafter We Go Again

At death the soul deserts its dwelling place
seeking a well-earned hibernating rest,
sorely needed before the next embrace
with humanity's newest life request
for rebirth and renewal's saving grace.

It seems a soul starts out as a blank slate
upon which life will write relentlessly
until death wipes it clean on that last date
losing all that it had gained, senselessly
to begin again with the whims of fate.

You have to wonder where it all will go,
all that lives in our imagination.
Where will attained wisdom finally flow?
Without which, the soul's reincarnation
seems to be a meaningless seed to sow.

JLO

January 2017

Hereafter Here – 55

~55~
Hereafter Here

Maybe at death we're still here.
They say immortals roam the land.
Ghosts take on all kinds of forms
still trying to live in this new way.
They never knew that when they went
they'd still be here, just different.

Imagine the billions who have died
since the beginning of time
watching each new day in life
forever lost as yet they linger.
Perhaps pining for what is gone,
a vicarious victory still to win.

If they exist but are senseless,
just a part of the world
like the sea or a tree,
you have to wonder what their life meant
if they have no power, no gaze, no wonder.
Forever forgotten, lost in the shadow,
nothing left to love or lament.

JLO

January 2017

~56~
Heavenly Hereafter

There might be an alternate universe.
It might be that place called heaven.
To another dimension that's quite a distance
you journey from life to boundless bliss.
You can't be sure, though it's often been said,
because to get there you must be quite dead.

So many questions of what to do there
in that place beyond imagination.
People often look up at talk of heaven
trying to see beyond space and time,
wondering if they really want to know
if heaven is where they're destined to go.

Of course, it could be a made-up myth.
We all want to think
there's a reason to exist,
to pray, to play, to yearn.
That we're not just some random spark
that flickers out when comes the dark.

If heaven exists it must be life's source
and not just a place to store energy
which Einstein said could never die.
But we like to think that it's perfection
where love will finally unite us all
in celebration of eternal thrall.

JAD

January 2017

Photo by author JoAnne Davis on vacation in Naples Florida 2019
Palm Tree – 57

-57-

Palm Tree

Your body might be smooth avocado
or perhaps have scales like brown artichokes
or bark like braided bread.
Handsome specimens will flaunt
carved necklaces of svelte ivory strips.

Almost always you dwell with your friends,
each waving their frond fans at the other.
Your fruited seed pods swell.
A signal that they are bursting with
a milky need to feed.

Daily you bow to the breeze
and know how to bend.
When adversity calls
you won't break
but stand tall again.

Paradise is yours.
Once you lived with Adam
and today live there still.
You radiate a certain glow
having greeted God so long ago.

JLO

February 2017

Winter's Deadly Beauty – 58

~58~
Winter's Deadly Beauty

Oh, it is so cold
in that deep dark jungle
called winter.

The freezing zero
of breathless air
suffocates.

Ice drips from the eaves
like tropical snakes
drooping from trees.

The sparkling beauty
of the jeweled landscape
tempts the senses
with deadliness.

J.L.O.

February 2017

~59~
The Double Sunshine

Standing on wooden planks
a long line patiently waits
to board the boat
for a sea-faring safari
on the Gulf,

to experience the soft kiss
of sea breezes
as the Double Sunshine stalks
the yachts and mansions
of the rich.

Seabirds perched on posts
eye the waves,
diving into the depths
for their sustenance
and a tourist's treat.

It's a watery way
to spend the day
skimming the sea's surface,
listening to the captain drone on,
to sit and sigh with pleasure.

But wait!
A sudden dark presence startles!
Swimming alongside the ship,
something jumps and reveals
its sleek, shiny self.

Playfully it leaps and rolls and splashes.
Excitement explodes. The soul brims
with hearts and flowers, diamonds and sunshine.
The world is suddenly a glorious place
full of amazing feelings of peace and joy.

Finally, the harbor beckons the boat,

now alive with island music,
the disembarkment awash with wonder.
In the deep, dark depths of the sea
the dolphin whispers a frothy farewell.

J.A.O.

February 2017

~60~
Fate's Fortune

Awaken at leisure
to stretches and kisses,
to another golden greeting
of warmth and light.

To be cared for
like a decadent sultana
ready to devour
raisin toast and tea.

To know the comfort
of loving arms that warm,
of the soothing satisfaction of safety
in a callous world.

Feel free to walk and talk at will,
to enjoy the soft breezes
and linger in that lavish
longing for life.

Watch the grass grow and know
that dinnertime approaches
when comes fulfillment of
hungering needs,

when sparkling water
quenches thirst
and allows wallowing
in cleanliness.

Sink deep into a featherbed
rocked by cozy comfort.
As the sun mingles with the moon
a mysterious black velvet cloak
finally flings open to reveal
the hidden jewels of the evening.

Eternity looms as the world turns.
Float on fantasy,
forever faithful
to fantastic fate.

J.A.Q.

February 2017

Sad Psyche – 61

~61~
Sad Psyche

There's a point that now needs to be made.
Though why that is I really can't say.
It's certainly time. I won't be swayed.
In order to know me you must learn
there's a sad side of me to discern.

Christmas is a lovely time of year
with surroundings gay and life so full
of laughter and love and all that's dear.
Yet ever since I was just a child
a present I knew was dread reviled.

At last, we're ready for New Year's Eve,
the season's final celebration.
Many guests were happily received
and a terrific time had by all.
Still 'twas into a hole I could crawl.

Who can't enjoy their vacation time,
like January in Florida?
Though filled with light and warmth and sunshine,
even then would my panic attack
until I'm home and I wish it back.

Though this might sound like a winter's thing
sadly, the truth is that it comes on
with almost every bump life can bring.
Whether the moment's joyful or sad
my psyche acts in a way that's bad.

So the point's been made and now you know
everything about my deepest dark.
Certainly never a secret though.
For I've never been able to hide
that sad part of me I can't abide.

February 2017

~62~
Pious Passion

I saw the poor and I prayed
for God to lift them away
that they might rise to riches,
never more to dig ditches.

I heard the hate being spewed
and wished God would see it slain.
If the ACLU sued
could a law prohibit pain?

I patted the bullied child's head
and said, "So sorry for your hurt.
Be sure to say a prayer each night
and everything will be all right."

There are victims of fire and flood
who need to clean up ash and mud.
They need to start over again.
O my God, please help them. Amen.

Every day brings the death of dreams.
Never give up. Keep on trying.
There's always a silver lining.
May God half-fill your glass again.

I am outraged and
I condemn.
But what is there to do?
My thoughts and prayers
are always with you.
God's will be done.
I hope He helps everyone.

March 2017

-63-

Serving King Tomorrow

A long time ago we all checked our cards,
each having holes meticulously carved
by machines designed to serve a master
who's king of a world vaster and faster.

A new millennium brought distraction
forcing this king's resourceful reaction.
We who were young always sweated and slaved,
trying to ensure the sovereign behaved.

Today we own watches, phones, and laptops.
The world's a carousel that never stops.
Every day I work. I have much to do.
There's always something new to fill the queue.

Chain gangs and blocks have had plenty of clout.
They were fine for a while there is no doubt.
But tomorrow starts a new music's note
which hopes to fulfill whatever we wrote.

There was a time when I was young
I gloried in that kingdom come.
Today though I serve tomorrow
with all the time I can borrow.

JLO

March 2017

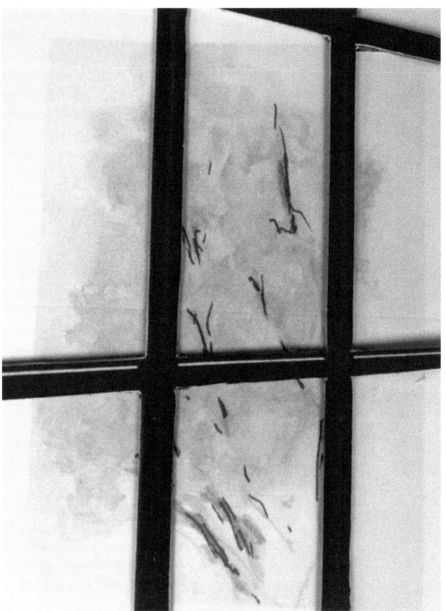

Picture Frame Life – 64

~64~
Picture Frame Life

There's a picture frame unknown
discovered by the restless one
who has no arms or legs for now
and looks for solace when alone.

Pressed up close, nose to nose,
awed by golden showers one day.
Magic that one never knows
unless the picture frame's exposed.

Through that frame this one sees
the very top of trees.
The seasons are only clear
for the part in this one's sphere.

Rooftops are what's most in sight,
swirling smoke from chimney tops.
Curtains of green change to gold
before the magic shower unfolds.

The stars are hidden as is the moon
beyond what that frame can tell.
When you have no arms or legs
still gratitude hangs on the wall.

The restless one sees sanity
presented on that picture frame.
This one knows for each day passed
there's yet another to outlast.

When you have no arms or legs
the picture frame portrays just part.
Someday one might live again.
The picture frame is hidden then.

J.A.Q.

March 2017

~65~
Journey to Destiny

stalking…stalking…stalking…stalking…stalking…stalking…stalk-
ing…stalking…stalking…s…
POUNCE!
The contented cub
dreams of destiny.

learning…learning…learning…learning…learning…learn-
ing…learning…learning…learning…
GROW!
Journey to the pinnacle
with your finely honed skills and powerful prowess.

feeding…feeding…feeding…feeding…feeding…feeding…feed-
ing…feeding…feeding…feed…
GORGE!
Devour even enervating experiences,
invaluable and irreplaceable.

seeking…seeking…seeking…seeking…seeking…seeking…seek-
ing…seeking…seeking… se…
HUNT!
Hard won wisdom springs forth
from adversity and sacrifice and persistence.

living…living…living…living…living…living…living…living…liv-
ing…living…living…liv…
BE!
Your time is now.
Your world awaits,
begging to begin.

Learn to linger in laughter.
Grow and graduate into prosperity.
Feed on freedom
and gorge on gratitude.
Seek to serve and
hunt for happiness.

Live to love and
be all that you can.

purring…purring…purring…purring…purring…purring…purr-
ing…purring…purring…purrin…
ROAR!
Awaken to destiny
O king of the jungle.

J.A.O.

March 2017

Weed Worthy – 66

~66~
Weed Worthy

There's a patch of ground
besieged by weeds
I never noticed before.
A gorgeous garden filled with flowers
will be my reward.
Backbreaking though it may be,
it's a scene worthwhile perceived.

There's a patch of ground
besieged by weeds
last week's rewarded scene.
A gorgeous garden filled with flowers
curse my neglect.
A few hours on bended knee,
spasms of stiffness withstood,
my worthiness perceived.

There's a patch of ground
besieged by weeds
another week gone by.
Again, hidden from sight,
I sit on cold hard ground
setting trowel to each rooted weed.
Bottom-numbing hours later,
a gorgeous garden filled with flowers perceived.

There's a patch of ground
besieged by weeds.
Week after week I work.
They have been a worthy foe
as we duel each seasoned hour.
I am done now. I perceive
the weeds have won at last.
A gorgeous garden filled with flowers weeps.

J.A.O.

April 2017

~67~
Face It

It's pitiful how badly you wanted this.
No one was more deserving.
I know you are distressed,
but do not cry.

Naively you hoped for a better outcome.
You tried your hardest.
Now you are feeling depressed,
sunk in sadness.

So unfair that your desires were not realized
though you did your due diligence.
As you dine on defeat,
try not to descend into the darkened depths.

For a lifetime you have craved distinction,
striven for success.
But now you have failed,
and weeping does not bring fulfillment.

Ironically, you thought you would achieve greatness
with your carefully cultivated confidence.
Your talents went unrecognized.
For your sorrow no one cares.

Embrace your mediocrity. Face it. Be done.
Or begin again your journey.
It's your choice.
Move over or move on.

JAD

April 2017

~68~
La-La Land

There's a place called La-La Land…
La-La Land… La-La Land…
It's a place where there's no pain…
there's no pain… there's no pain…
It might start with a pulled tooth…
a pulled tooth… a pulled tooth…
Or perhaps some broken bones…
broken bones… broken bones…
Then they give you pills to pop…
pills to pop… pills to pop…
Soon you start to feel better…
feel better… feel better…
In a place where there's no pain…
there's no pain… there's no pain…
No more tears in La-La Land…
La-La Land… La-La Land…
'Til it's time to come back home…
come back home… come back home…
Save some pills for the next trip…
the next trip… the next trip…
When you can't find happiness…
happiness… happiness…
When your life is just too hard…
just too hard… just too hard…
When there's pain that won't refrain….
won't refrain… won't refrain…
La-La Land will beckon you…
beckon you… beckon you…
Then you're lost in La-La Land…
La-La Land… La-La land…
then you're lost… then you're lost…

JLO

April 2017

Paths – 69

-69-
Paths

Walk the path.
Keep treading on
to nowhere

until it's back-up time
to a line
before the brambles began.

Maybe there's another way,
painstakingly to be forged,
with an end in sight.

Pound that new path.
It might become the gateway
leading to old beginnings.

J.A.O.

August 2017

~70~
Slippers

Always they were cold,
so very numb they never noticed
their toes' frozen franticness.
Into that sad state enter
blue polka-dotted white
pockets of warm refuge

that envelop the freezing
feet screaming for relief.
Finally, they slide home
into their stride.
Though the cold still lurks
in dim needles and pins

those fleet feet ignore.
Instead, they savor the warmth
into which their toes are snuggled.
Savior slippers that
shuffle them down
the slippery slope of life.

JSD

August 2017

Modern Art – 71

~71~
Modern Art

Start with a square
which really won't do.
Intercept with a circle
representing
the infinity of existence
of course.

For the whole experience,
triangles are needed,
angled this way and that.
Each might hold new shapes
or stand alone
in domination.

Draw some circles within circles
perhaps to represent eyes,
an egg sunny side up,
an eclipse of the sun.
Color vibrantly
for a monochrome look.

It is up to others to find the heart, the brain,
arms, legs, and liver.
Or to discover a fruit tree
or a violin.
The infinity of existence
hides within an imagination of paint.

Critics say there's no point or purpose
perceived or understood.
But curiosity is a connoisseur
and the mundane sometimes will mutate.
Whoever is up to the search
will often find that which they seek.

August 2017

~72~
Goodbye

Oh hush!
We know
it's time
for you
to go.
It's sad.
(We weep.)
But true.
(We're calm.)
It's done.
(We're fine.)
Don't wait.
Just go.

JAD.

August 2017

Dining Room Table – 73

-73-
Dining Room Table

Made in America
by skilled Amish craftsmen
who dwell along
the Appalachian Trail abiding
in that old fashioned way.

It gleams…

The years passed, full
of endless moving
and mischievous children,
hidden scars of carved names,
hot cups of lemon tea.

It serves…

Loneliness now admires
the bogus bouquet carefully centered.
Day after day,
no one dines
on this table of time.

It grieves…

Crafted for the ages,
the table awaits
meals to be served
to mischievous children
hungering for their future.

It knows…

All mourning has finished,
a few more scars to be earned.

It endures…

JAO

August 2017

~74~
Deep

I look into your eyes
and behold
the depths of the universe
where every thought
might be delved,
every wish fulfilled.

But first one must dive
into the abyss,
maneuver each alley,
sail though life's blood
looking to land some
bare-boned sense.

There is always trouble.
Each canyon and gorge
is filled with fear.
Fly from that first sign
though escape cannot be planned
and resistance is futile.

Every path leads to loss,
binding body and brain in knots.
Might as well submerge yourself in it.
The meaning of life is deep,
so jump into the foaming sea
and feed the fish.

JJ.D.

August 2017

Tiny Bits – 75

-75-
Tiny Bits

Trudge the blizzarding snow
with stubborn forbearance,
through the crunchy cold, the brittle freeze,
remembering snow angels
and sweetly scented grass.

Though resigned to suffer the gloom
of putrid pretense
sanity still sparkles in the
shimmering suspense
of a misty dawn.

Sorrow comes,
the inescapable weeping time.
Yet each breath of air caresses,
and the buds of nature
continue to explode.

We eat, we sleep,
live, learn, laugh, and love.
The world continues to twist, to turn.
Still there are those tiny bits,
serenity out of time.

JLD

September 2017

~76~
I Never Met Him

He was a man I never met
but always thought I knew.
I'd heard of him for years and years.
I knew his sister well.
She said he had stories to tell,
ones that made for happy tears,
that he might someday sell.

He was a man I never knew
yet admired through the years.
He seemed so very confident
from everything I'd heard.
He had ideas he thought ideal
and was not afraid to try
what some might deem absurd.

He was a man I never knew.
Nor did we ever meet.
I pitied him for being lost
but envied what he'd found.
To me it seemed he had it all.
Dreaming dreams, he followed through,
he never counted cost.

He was a man I never met.
Though I knew he was someone
I always yearned to be.
There were times when he was lost,
whereas I was always found.
Still, I thought he had it all
and all I had was me.

September 2017

~77~
I Said So

There's not much to say
that might make you listen.
Who am I, after all?
Just a sayer
with something to say.

I might say you're wrong,
give all the reasons why.
But who am I, after all?
Just a sayer
whose timing's awry.

I might say you're right
though I can't explain why.
Of course, the world now listens
to a sayer
who's learned how to lie.

September 2017

Almost Here – 78

-78-

Almost Here

It's coming. A wish in the air,
a whispered hint
of beckoning glory.
Though babyhood has sadly passed
the young child instills glee.

Who can resist?
It's coming.
Aromas of sun-bladed green
intertwined with lilac,
the peony still in bud.

I hold my breath. It's coming.
Graduates march onward.
Baby birds flap world-ready wings.
Soon-to-be-brides ardently await
the June of their lives.

The maypole still dances
in acknowledgement of ancient ritual.
Summer of youth.
Summer of dreams.
Summer of sentiment.

The sun journeys higher,
spring's hope to soon arrive.
All yearning is resurrected
for that perfect summer's day.
It's coming!

JLO

September 2017

Symphony Refrained – 79

~79~

Symphony Refrained

Once upon a time
there was a place
where we could go,
me and all that I am,
to a symphony refrained
by my mind's concerto.

Once upon a time
I knew how to dance.
I could sing for hours
just to hear myself
vying for your existence,
my soprano to your alto.

I have sought your truths
where I keep my yesterdays,
where my futures are hiding.
I know this song and I love it.
The chorus makes me cry
and laugh and sing.

There are new melodies now
waiting to be found.
I keep myself open
to hear your new notes dancing.
The music is mine,
now and once upon a time.

JA.O.

February 2018

~80~
Puddle Jumping

Observe the little ones running free.
They wander in the wind,
rendezvous with rain.
Mischievous pre-pubescence
well accustomed to the bliss,
indulge the wet.
They may disregard their baths
but beg to shower in raindrops.

Sun pours through the clouds
creating a rainbow of wealth.
Hold the drops, the mist,
close to your childish breast
before their shadows slip
free from your wildness.
Pools of water are everywhere
which only fools avoid.

There are always those
to tiptoe the edges,
but most are eager, unrestrained.
Ready to pounce, to jump
as hard and fast as possible,
soaking themselves and splashing
all silly enough to be
standing on the sidelines.

February 2018

~81~

I See You

You sit there
and I see you
when we all come together
as we have for years.
Each still trying to know the other,
thinking we already do.

I thought I knew you,
my consensus from long ago.
Then we had a conversation
in the garden
and now I must acknowledge
I was unaware.

We discussed God
and death and weeds.
We spoke of our doubts,
our anxieties and our blisters.
You seemed so full of confidence
but I had forgotten

about the hiding,
the crying under the skin.
You think you know someone
but find you never did.
You think you know yourself
yet again find you know nothing.

JAO

February 2018

~82~
State of Mine

Settled third of the first thirteen,
we always knew with freedom came
a reason to work together,
to never rest on laurels past,
but keep on striving to create
growth, strength, and vigor in my state.

We keep our public schools first rate
to satisfy the seeking mind.
Learn for fun or a future's need,
there's something to suit everyone.
So, keep in mind it's not too late.
"The sky's the limit" in my state!

Our winters highlight sports and snow
'til lilacs grow and bluebirds trill.
Summers will feature fairs and fests
though apple-picking might be best.
Every season will illustrate
the awesome wonder of my state.

Hike the mountains, hills, and valleys.
Choose rivers, lakes, or ocean swims.
Don't forget to explore the parks,
theatre, concerts, all the arts.
For wholesome fun don't hesitate
to enjoy life's zest in my state.

An educated populace,
transportation, technology
and our natural resources
are reasons we're so passionate,
so ready to accommodate
every citizen in my state.

I know this sounds a bit too trite
yet it's the truth though I admit

there's always room for improvement.
Yes, for sure we have more to do.
Still, I feel blessed that it's my fate
to live and love in New York State.

J.A.Q.

February 2018

~83~

Cliché

You reach beyond time
to touch totality
until everyone realizes
how common you are.
Yet they embrace you
in all your comfort,
centered in an existence
where only the cynical
might mention your weariness.
All others adore your innocence
steeped in inspiration.

Education is key
to teach the sea,
each blade of grass
and blink of star,
animal minds
imbedded in instinct.
Even the vegetables
will scream.
You are so maddeningly present.
But should mercy prevail
or be lost in derision?

You are everywhere
and were created
in vibrant clarity,
beloved for your brilliance.
Now you are an emperor
so replete in your power
you need no clothing.
The cynical might notice
and cry that the emperor wears no clothing
but no one cares
because you are so lovely.

April 2018

~84~
Tattooed Gardener

Those old red, pink, and white,
the indisputable ink of spring,
Uncle Bill made sure
his prized peonies imprinted
permanent beauty marks
that seared my tender soul.

In summer's parlor I acquired
that Blaze of Rose design.
Dripping red jewels festooned
the long rickety white trellis in our front yard,
a Norman Rockwell picture perfect spectacle.
I chose the best of buds
to carefully cut and carry forth,
my goodwill's gift to give.

Up a long block of hill I would wander
when my mother wasn't looking,
to the deep woods she had so clearly forbidden.
My guilt decided to never go again
until I came upon a dot of sky,
a patch of bright where rays poured down.
Forever carved into my astonished eye
I saw wildflowers of every kind.

In that time, we butter-cupped each other's chins
and daisies were destroyed for love.
Those stalwart weeds along the highway,
daylily, Queen Anne's lace, wild phlox, and others,
I always yearned to pick but sadly never did.
One huge lilac with branches bent low
formed a small womb-like structure
where deep within we needled our imaginations.

Today I plant and weed and watch,
marveling at each tattoo pressed upon my dreams.
Weaving through tangled paths of youth and years

through memory's maze of mangled moments
my life's art decorates every crease and crevice in
this garden's parlor of hope and pain and ink.

J.A.O.

June 2018

Photo by author JoAnne Davis on vacation in Naples Florida 2015
Sunset on a Florida Beach – 85

~85~
Sunset on a Florida Beach

Time in paradise stands still
waiting for deliverance
from each impatient moment
that arrived early
to play in the sand.

The passing hours build up
into a lump within my throat,
choking me with grief and regrets
and awe, as I am overwhelmed with
this panorama of celestial brilliance.

Our star's blazing bow is nearly finished,
its partner's pirouette complete.
I sigh as the sea swallows
that last golden glow
and finally gulps the pearlescent twilight.

Shimmering tears of my soul
shed into the darkness,
impatient time weeps with me.
We both know today's essence is gone,
forever lost in the sand.

September 2018

Sixteen – 86

~86~
Sixteen

It began with your essence
when the first silky knot was tied.
Then your body's form was born
to anchor and to bind
with a world born anew
wrapping you
in protective sustenance.

Body and world
patiently pupate together.
With the threaded needle of life
you are painstakingly stitched,
experience by experience,
until entirely engulfed
in your childhood cocoon,
continually spinning
comfort and home,
cozy and warm,
around you.

Tighter and tighter it wraps.
Pushing and pulling it pulses,
with unbearable tension
as comfort becomes cramped
and you can't go back
because body and soul beg
for escape,
for the inevitable eruption,
be it riotous or restrained.
The drama, the thrill, the need
to emerge from your chrysalis,
to be finally born
into yourself.

JAO

January 2020

~87~
Once Upon a Time

Once upon a time
I had a sweetheart.
We wed and lived our lives fine.
Up until now
when confusion took over.
We lost our storybook line.

For instance,
he says he's my husband.
But I worry
because I am no longer sure.
Maybe he is and maybe he isn't.
Not knowing is hard to endure.

So I try to stay sane
in this quandary of fate
where everyone tells me
there's no need for fright.
As long as we are together
then everything should be all right

until tomorrow
when all will have forgotten
who I am
and who he is to me.
Yet I will be offered reassurance
about now and once upon a time.

January 2020

~88~
Life's Delight

There's a song on the radio
when you tune in the top twenty
or change to a classical channel,
switch to swing, blues, or country.

Everything on TV is instrumental,
game shows, suspense, drama, and comedy,
even shows of reality,
sometimes so subliminal
the music in the message is missed.

The tunes are in technology.
On YouTube, smart phones, and more
are resonating refrains
recorded for posterity.

While out in our world
the wind whistles.
Trees rustle to their rhythm.
Birds chirp, cheep, peck, and hum.
A chorus of locusts
sings for sunset
and peepers for dawn.
The storms play percussion
with thunder like the crash of cymbals
and raindrops pounding
earth's ancient drum.
Yes. There's music in nature,
sung to life's delight.

There's a melody in my head,
haunting and hypnotic.
A lullaby lives inside me
to croon out soothing notes,
a balm to calm my stress.
Harmony inhabits my hands
as they clap in synchroneity

to the tunes in my toes
each tapping together a dance.
There's music in my heart.
It's called the beat of life.
There's a song in my soul
sung for God alone.

J.A.O.

January 2020

My Personal Awe's List – 89

~89~
My Personal Awe's List

Bluebirds have always been huge for me,
and their eggs,
and their nests,
orioles because I hardly ever see them,
hummingbirds so tiny and fragile and strong,
cardinals and robins, chickadees, goldfinches, and more,
I also adore.

I am always delighted by dolphins,
intrigued by mysteries of the moon.
There's inspiration in the sun's rise and set.

Exotic Maui, is memorable,
fantastic and far,
wondrous and breathtaking and awesome.

As for the Grand Canyon there are no words,
other world, nether world, outer world so vast.

Then there are the trees in all their glory,
life, death, resurrection
their unending story.

Christmas Eve magic,
midnight mass music.

Seeds grow to beauty.
Seeds grow to dinner.
Seeds grow to babies.
What could be
more amazing than that?

Excellence and talent
my heart and brain embrace.
Nourishing and flourishing of life
like a flame.
The speed of time,

so slow I wait in agony,
so swift it runs out.
The journey from youth to old age,
as the torch passes
from one generation to the next.
How time heals heartache
with new chapters in life.
Kindness and empathy never grow old,
and so rare to find anywhere is
unconditional love.

J.S.D.

January 2020

Magnolia Bush – 90

~90~
Magnolia Bush

Hiding in a bush's beauty
are birds humming
their hymn of serenity and bliss
as they flit and they feast
on sugar water and nectar.
So happy each hum drum day,
oblivious to the threat of
snake and hawk

as the latter lurk about their prey
stalking a different sort of survival.
The hawk will swoop unexpectedly.
The snake will sneakily slither.
Always ravenous, they
hungrily seek to devour
innocence hidden in a
magnolia thicket.

The peril is real
and will take its toll.
But contentment reigns.
Still the promised refuge
where love and courage prevail
while harmony hums on
a protective bush
and everyone feels at home.

January 2020

~91~
Age-Old Resolution

The seven trumpets blare,
heralding another new decade.
The last hurrah
to harness happiness,
acclaim possibilities,
and deny destiny
for septuagenarians
steeped in determination
to slow down certainty.

Gray hairs and blue hairs,
white hairs and no hairs
prepare to participate
in their quest for new zest.
The fit may just tread
up the steep hill to hope
while the clumsy will crawl
and claw through resolutions
made of drunken desire
and Auld Lang Syne.

January 2020

~92~
Lady Bountiful

She lay at her last hour
reminiscing:
How beautiful I was,
she thought.
How fashionable my senses,
a supernova for my time.

I trended up to the moment.
Every woman envied me.
Every man desired me,
quintessence of fantasy.

Peaches and cream were my cheeks.
They glowed sunshine.
My crowning glory,
like a flaming sunset.
Eyes that reflect the blue-green seas
deep enough to drown in.
Lavish lips pursed in pout.
Soft mounds of cream the blossoming
touch to my body's perfection.

Dressmakers and designers
begged for my attentions.
High heeled leather
loved my tiny feet.

Such a gift I have been
to all who have longed.
I cry for you
as I breathe my last.
Now it is time for us to part.
Forgive me if you choose.
Forget me if you can.

February 2020

~93~
Fear of Fire

TheMultitude: Roasting marshmallows sitting around a campfire,
relaxing.

Me: Hesitantly I strike a match with no luck.

TheMultitude: Hamburgers and hot dogs at a hot summer day's barbeque,
fun.

Me: Dubiously I drag the match across its flint. Nothing.

TheMultitude: Fourth of July fireworks,
thrilling.

Me: Shocking success! I quickly drop the flaming stick.

TheMultitude: Make a wish and blow out the candles.
We made it another year!

Me:
I once saw a house on fire.
Total devastation.

I once saw a man engulfed in alcoholic flame.
Unbearably horrific.

I have been singed.
I have been scorched.
I have been charred.
I have been scarred.
I have been burned!

Fire is a ferocious phenomenon.

The fear devours me.

JLD

February 2020

~94~
It's All Good

Crank up the music
to bring home my past.
The Beatles and Beach Boys
among all the others
were part of
an unforgettable youth.
They participated in
my poignant blisses.
They comforted me
through crazy bumps
as I twisted in chains
that restrained my needs,
my wants,
myself.

Crank up the music
to 1000 decibels.
Let Elvis and Neil
block out and overcome
that unlamented time
where hurt and pain,
and pride
buried me in anger
and recrimination
and shame.
It was what it was,
and it's over.

Crank up the music.
Adele and Abba now soothe
my present
and perhaps my future
which will soon be my past.
Today I live in a different sphere
where the past
might be regretted or revered,

or not.
Where all has become good.
Today I am bound to my children
and my children's children
and they to me.
We are now one. (I won!)
Crank up the music!

J.L.O.

February 2020

~95~
Honor

To lie or not to lie,
to cheat or not to cheat,
to judge or not to judge,
to love or not to love,
every day's a test
to try one's best.

Sometimes the difference
one tries to make
might seem invisible.
Sometimes the only
thing to be won is loss
of your last chance.

Still, honor may reside
in an ordinary existence
lived stubbornly,
where one would never
give up the integrity
embedded from the beginning.

February 2020

~96~
Hermit Crab

Hiding in a moon closet
or exposure to the dark,
retracting in sunlight
to a snug and warm safe sanctum.
Back in that shell of self
until decisions need be made
to be a shell-shocked social being
or be shell-locked alone.

Life is the aquarium
with sea waters nearby.
There is sand in which to burrow.
There are shells in which to bide.
Sustenance abounds
to tempt a hungry soul.
There is respite to be found
in living life alone.

So many shells
from which to choose
a succor and a freedom
when loneliness ensues.
Sometimes all that's there
is hidden nakedness.
Other times expose
all that vulnerability knows.

Once these homes
meant shelter,
a place to raise a future.
Now they are comfort,
a place to linger
in solitary splendor
to await the final tides
that will wash everything clean.

March 2020

~97~
The Travelers

The man and woman sit together
on a bench at the mall.
The woman is on her smart phone,
fingertips frantically flying
with the world wide web spread
open to her gaze.
The man is people watching.

A suicide bomber decimates a playground in Pakistan.
A hospital has admitted another gunshot victim in Syracuse.
Presidential candidates are bickering.

Teenagers call obnoxious taunts to each other.
A flock of Canadian tourists trample the food court.
An elderly man with a cane attempts the stairs.

The woman finally rises with a tired smile
as does the man.
Holding hands, they stroll to the nearest café.
Sitting together at their table
each goes out again into their world
where they bear weary witness
to the exhaustion of travels untrodden.

JS.D

March 2020

-98-

Back Seat Driver

Be careful! Watch it!
...Backing up!
You're not going straight enough!
Don't race
to make that light!
You are tailgating!
...Too close!
Someone is tailgating you!
Please pull over!
You are not supposed to...
pass on a double solid line.
Don't speed
just because you're passing!
I swear you speed to catch up...
just so you can pass!

Be careful! Watch it!
That guy is on his phone.
Don't beep your horn!
Someone could come with road rage.
Stop speeding!
Stop tailgating!
You should be...
in the other lane.
Stop veering
into the other lane.
Why do you have to pass
every truck you see?
A truck is coming on!
Move over for heaven sakes!

Be careful! Watch it!
You wouldn't do that...
if a police officer was behind us.
You'd be mad
if I drove like that!

You parked too far…
from the curb!
You didn't pull in…
far enough!
Your front end…
is sticking out.
Your back end…
is sticking out.
Please keep both hands…
on the wheel!

That guy is driving crazy!
Please get away
from him…

JLO

March 2020

This New Spring – 99

~99~
This New Spring

The ancient journey advances
south to north
agonizingly slow until finally
the fulfillment of our primordial need
for annual resurrection.
But now comes a swifter journey
east to west
bringing heartache and fear,
a new invasion
perceived in kaleidoscopes of color,
hope and despair conjoined.

Yet Spring marches onward.
Snowdrops poke through the snow
and narcissus nod
as robins bob.
Frantic forsythias explode in goldenness
while a foe flies in from afar.
Stealthily the assassin
subdues the earth
like a late frost upon the lilac,
hail on hosta.
Still, Spring survives despite it all.

It is we who huddle, who hide
from this new spring.
Slowly we fold, we fade
back into a dark age
deep into a dark time.
Longing has turned into
a leprosy of sorts.
The kaleidoscope now
covers the sun.
Its strength overpowers.
Its savagery overwhelms.

JAO

April 2020

~100~
Still...

Even as you stretched out your arms
to give a hand,
you pretended to be indifferent.

You have said that your neighbor
is not your problem,
yet I have sensed rescue.

Despite your disdain for diplomacy,
your derision of naivete, of trust,
despite cynicism,

a widow is consoled,
someone's son advised.
Yesterday a daughter was coddled,
today a sibling supported.

What is that all about?
Perhaps I don't know
what I'm talking about.

Still... peace be with you...

as you live in denial
and scorn civility.

JSD

July 2020

~101~
Uneasy

They are rioting in the streets.
Children clamor about calamities to come.
My book had a poor ending
and the beaches are closed—
blue algae, e-coli, or Covid, I forget.

Who am I but a speck?
Can a speck be a giant?
We all have our priorities
but they are now pointless
and my mind is uneasy.

For forever have I feigned calm.
I consider consequences.
Calling for baby step solutions
I soothe doubters.
I scoff at those who give up.

But I am lost, lost, lost…
My heart pounds,
blood pressure raised.
The dread drains my marrow.
The future is relentless.

July 2020

~102~
Congratulations

For

just a few years ago the
aloneness was real in a land of lingering lack.
Yesterday was searching for tomorrow,
meandering the countryside 'til
etchings of possibility hinted at
satisfaction and wisdom to come.

And

now there is a fresh outlook
in a new land of loyalty.
Now there is a today to savor,
a new future to foresee.

And now also

breathtakingly he arrives, ready to
ravage head, home, and heart, so
overwhelming, so fulfilling. Though there are
obstacles still to be overcome, it is obvious that the
key has finally been found to unlock
satisfaction and wisdom, now blended and hardened into one.

J.S.D.

July 2020

~103~
Animal Shelter

An oasis exists,
haven of bonhomie,
understatement of need,
where each caged creature
glimpses him or herself
in the other,
escapees all
from squalor's taint.

Hurt hungers for rescue.
Comfort confronts pain.
Cleanliness is a concern
since filth and disease are commonplace.
Perhaps their endings will be happy ones.
Or perhaps not. It's a toss-up.
Society will debate
and decide.

JA.D.

September 2020

~104~
Play Ball

Just not in the streets.
Remember to toss high for the serve,
to kick long and hard for the goal.
Watch out for windows and water and
keep at least one eye on the ball.
A win is always well and good of course,
but never forget the fun.
Enjoy the game.

JLD

November 2021

-105-
Memories of Mom

My mom told me to do my best.
I thought her words were just a jest.
I didn't see.
It took more living to suggest
why that might be.
My pride would always need a test
my mom told me.

My mom told me about her past.
Her experiences were vast.
From her story,
sixteen children, she was the last
of so many.
It seems she grew up way too fast
my mom told me.

My mom told me that being poor
was something she had to endure—
no other way.
But for her children she was sure
we'd be ready.
For us she wished a life grandeur
my mom told me.

My mom told me she loved to shop.
She said she would until she'd drop.
She said that we
could have some fun yet be on top
fashionably.
It feels so good to have that prop
my mom told me.

My mom told me she'd clean my house.
I didn't even need to rouse.
She was happy
taking care of me and my spouse.
Don't be silly.
I like to help so please don't grouse
my mom told me.

My mom told me she cooked us meals.
She knew that food always appeals.
She knew that we
would remember how good it feels
and that is why
sometimes the stomach seals the deals
my mom told me.

My mom told me that school was good.
She would have finished if she could.
You're so lucky.
She made sure you knew where she stood.
Learn properly.
It's necessary and you should
my mom told me.

My mom told me I made my bed.
There's nothing I could do instead.
It shouldn't be.
For all the tears I might have shed,
Futility.
Keep on living. Forget the dread
my mom told me.

My mom told me on our phone call
about many cuts that did befall,
that hurt badly.
We discussed it all, big and small
so readily.

Sometimes our talks would make her bawl
my mom told me.

My mom told me while we gardened
all those things she never pardoned,
so lucky me,
every thought that she had darkened
was there to see.
Speaking freely made her heartened
my mom told me.

My mom told me that Saturdays
would keep us together always
as family,
to experience fun and frays
like a party.
There's enjoyment in in all these ways
my mom told me.

My mom told me she sacrificed.
For love's sake she hadn't thought twice.
With certainty
every last thing was overpriced.
Insanity.
Any mercy would have sufficed
my mom told me.

My mom told me to cope with loss
so terrible you cannot gloss—
feign it away.
You must be careful not to cross
to lunacy.
What people think don't give a toss
my mom told me.

My mom told me her life would end

but until then she'd be my friend,
and we'd have tea.
She explained how she would depend
on family.
So, look for calls that she would send
my mom told me.

My mom told me I shouldn't cry
since that's the way the world goes by.
So do not plea.
Stop begging her to try to fly
from destiny.
When it's the time just let her die.
My mom told me.

JSD

January 2022

The Western Sky – 106

~106~

The Western Sky

In time's journey
as I dreamed,
in years that wished me well
eagerness gleamed.
Need makes for hope
that lives deep in the heart
from where one should not flee.

Like a gate swinging open beckons
truth will set me free.
When the sun sets in the western sky
stars will set me free.

In the still of morn
in one life of day
in every song of birds
the gentle will bring
sweetness in words.
As the humble know
it should be every plea.

Like a gate swinging open beckons
truth will set me free.
When the sun sets in the western sky
stars will set me free.

Dance in rainbow rays.
Dance in bliss.
Nature begins to grow
with the universe's kiss.
Yes, let it grow.
A mind is amazing
when it's allowed to roam.

Like a gate swinging open beckons
truth will bring me home.
When the sun sets in the western sky
stars will bring me home.

January 2022

~107~
Pillow Talk

We need to sleep…
don't have much time
before the little one stirs.
I think it's your turn…
or maybe it's mine.
Doesn't matter…
we'll both be woken and worn.

Will you come to the party
at my work next week?
Don't know… don't want to…
such a waste of time.
Those people don't care…
and I just can't bear
their points of view.

But I need you there…
I hope to go places…
We need to be seen…
Yes, I know what you mean.
But I'm tired…
not social…
my own work demands.

What about our children…?
We must raise them up right.
We won't have them long…
and they need our support.
Their lives already changing…
we will figure it out.
We will not fall short.

Work was hard today…
Someone took credit…
until it all fell through.
Can't wait for the time…
hopefully soon…

when daily duties slow down,
when our dreams come true.

Yes, I absolutely agree
with all that you say
but for now
it's time to sleep.
I'm tired. I have a headache.
My back aches too
and I have so much to do.

J.A.Q.

January 2022

~108~
Curiosity

Curiosity came calling.
I followed where she led
and she brought me
into myself
to tease my tender core.

Yearning now beckons me
with impossible views.
Some that caught my eye
and held, digging deep,
holding tight, changing me.

If opportunity next comes knocking
I cannot be sure though I must decide
if I am ready for what might follow,
the relishing of a curious dream
or yearning desire finally realized.

January 2022

~109~
Gulliver

From the beginning
ever restless and bored,
the urge was relentless,
too much to ignore.
Immerse yourself in pretense
if that's what it takes,
or an escape to distraction
might be your chosen hook
to the plane, train, bus, or book.

In some places you feel tiny.
In some places you feel tall.
Will any place make you happy?
Or do you just stall?
You live for the magic.
You live for the gain.
Be it by plane, train, bus, or book,
it's out there somewhere,
that brighter outlook.

So hard to come home.
So hard to be real.
So hard to fit in.
Where is the pleasure?
Where is the pain?
When boredom befalls,
or regret has you shook,
there's always the plane,
the train, the bus, or the book.

J.A.O.

February 2022

~110~
The Wolf

On the precipice he stands,
proud posture pitched forward,
shaggy pelt rustling.
He reminisces…
of playful puppy pack time…
Cool grasses…
Deep snow…
Hills and valleys…
Exuberance!

Curiosity carries on
as he probes,
participates in a
saga of survival.
Loyalty absolute,
courage in abundance,
instincts highly honed,
skills ever evolving
in a recipe for future
happiness and harmony.

He howls determination.
He howls knowledge.
He howls to let the world
know his readiness
for what is to come.
His pack filled with pride,
he stands on the cusp,
eager to leap into the unknown,
eager to leap into destiny.

J.S.D.

February 2022

~111~
Light the Way

Light the way, wise ones,
for our lost land
where some whisper
the future seeks light.
Others will warn
the future seeks hope.
With guidance from wise ones
future can cope.

J.L.O.

May 2022

~112~

Listen, Listen, Maestro Man

Listen, listen, maestro man.
With great care you formed a plan
to ensure your students grow
as they make their music flow.

Horns and drums and flutes and more,
a cheerful din to explore.
Blues, folk, classical and rock,
listen, listen, jazz and Bach.

Each new year a novice class,
from the keyboard to the brass.
You know it's time to instruct.
You know it's time to conduct.

Ever patient, firm, and kind,
and much more, all intertwined.
As maestro you are the one
to make sure the work gets done.

When they finally performed,
then you watched them be transformed.
Look what happened with your plan!
Listen, listen, maestro man.

JSD

May 2022

-113-
Blank Slate

A blank slate tempts,
laying siege
to sanity,

testing patience
and endurance
with endless chances
to be wrong.

To start seems easy, enticing,
the entrancement of deception,
where a careless move might beget
the beginning of a bad end

and recovery is not guaranteed because
there is disaster in the details.
So, mind the minutiae
with unwavering attention

until finally a finish is found
somewhere at the crossroads
of acceptance and denial,
of a dream and reality.

Then take some time to savor
the heights, basking in
a fleeting moment of
effervescent euphoria,

or to wallow in the depths,
in a grim determination
to start over,
the stark obsessive necessity.

One way or another,
a blank slate, pure and clean,
is irresistible temptation.

June 2022

Standing Engagement – 114

~114~
Standing Engagement

The curtain opens
with sun, sky, and earth in place,
eternal super
stars. The stage is set, ready.
It's time. The show must go on.
And the trees are there.

Snowdrops play warmup.
Songbirds sing while blue bells dance
in the gentle breeze.
See the new leaves, dew-speckled!
Lilacs! Dandelion fluff!
And the trees stand straight.

The wind will whip up
amid rumbles of thunder
and lightning flashes.
The rain pounds down. The drama!
All who thirst have been assuaged.
And the trees stand guard.

No intermission.
Roses, lilies, daisies bow,
showing off beauty.
The sun, the sky, and the earth,
perfect backdrop to it all.
And the trees stand tall.

They each have their part,
sage, mint, violets and more,
as they take their time
to shine, one vying with the
other to be reigning star.
And the trees stand strong.

Days grow short and leaves
show off their blazing colors
before drifting down
to the earth ready to rest.
The curtain closes for now.
And the trees still stand.

J.S.D.

June 2022

~115~
An Ocean of Tears

An ocean overflows,
spilling its essence

in pounding waves of anguish,
for the anxiety and the despair,
for the fear and the anger and the shame,
for the futility,
for the lost innocence,

in cascading waves of celebration,
for the accomplishments,
for the special occasions,
for art and music,
for laughter and love,

in surging waves of jubilation,
for the abilities,
for the everyday joys,
for the triumphs,
for being alive,

in salty waves
pouring from my eyes,
choking me,
drowning me.

August 2022

~116~
Big Box

The portal glides open
granting access to a realm
resolute in its mission
to satisfy need and want.
A realm facetiously
known as Big Box.

Indeed, a kingdom contained,
a second home to many
with an allure hard to deny.

Almost anything can be found there.

A pauper finds a bit to stave off hunger.

The middle finds comfort in toothpaste,
pots and pans and proof
of their subsistence.

A place where workers feel captive
in perceived servitude,
yearning to leave the leash,
to escape to a greener side
as they search for substance.

And the prosperous sneer
as they outbid each other's stake,

reveling in this other world
where profits skyrocket
from third world's labor
and first world's frenzy.
Where the kings of both worlds
sup up with greed.

August 2022

~117~
Clean House

Once we lived in
a newly built house,
sparkling and spotless.
In my delusions I thought
it would always be clean,
until I began to realize
just living causes dirt.
So, we tried to live lightly.

Still, dust balls and cobwebs multiplied.
Porcelain bowls turned foul.
Though shoes had long been banned,
the floors were already sullied
with scuff marks and muck.
Appliances once shiny, now smudged
despite attempts never to touch
with bare fingers.

Now we live in a different house
bedraggled by ninety years
of existing and subsisting.
An old, dirtied home
seems so much cleaner
than the sparkling one
that sadly dirtied itself
despite its pristine beginning.

August 2022

Tribute to the Peony – 118

~118~
Tribute to the Peony

Who welcomes in the month of June,
a sign that summer will come soon?

The beauteous peony!

For weeds and bugs, they've not a care
and there's no disease that would dare.
It has already been acclaimed
for robust vigor they are named.

The eye-catching peony!

Ants will savor distended buds,
balls of nectar from which blooms burst
in white or red, all shades between,
from petals few to those umpteen.

The remarkable peony!

Who is beloved from East to West?
Who lives so long that they are blessed?
Their scent is sweet and strong and so
reminiscent of long ago.

The extraordinary peony!

They were Uncle Bill's favorite
so, on his grave we planted it.

The peony!

August 2022

~119~
Awakenings

Waiting…
in this warm cozy place
with my knees folded into my chest.
Though I wish I could remain
here, living pleasantly in limbo,
I await my awakening
into light
and life.

Waiting…
in my crisp new clothes,
my hair so carefully combed.
With pencils and papers and books
and lunch packed into a book bag
I await my awakening
into knowledge
and the meaning of life.

Waiting…
to fill out an application,
to be interviewed and chosen,
to start my first day,
to be independent.
I await my awakening
into security
and the meaning of money.

Waiting…
in a church redolent with incense
where the candles glow and
flowers adorn the white-carpeted aisle.
Before the alter we stand where
I await my awakening
into connubiality
and the meaning of love.

Waiting…
while I attend to daily routines,
while I garden and I read and I write,
while I enjoy each new season,
while I wallow in life,
I await my awakening
into knowledge,
into security,
into love,
into eternal life.

JLO

September 2022

Imagination's Tutor – 120

~120~
Imagination's Tutor

This traveler will venture out
into a past, into a future,
into universes, parallel or present,
into the unknown.
With so many possibilities,
with so much meaning and magic,
her imagination is impeccable.
Her earth knows no bounds,
her cosmos, incalculable.

She has been the hero
risking everything,
the one who saves others.
Or the realist,
the one who saves herself.
Or perhaps the villain,
who saves nobody.

Mystery, mystical, romance or fantasy.
Maybe a princess, maybe a pauper,
a scientist or astronaut.
Sometimes powerful.
Sometimes impotent.
Always fantastic, always engrossing.
The printed page will transport.
The printed page will tutor because

her imagination is her story.
Call it her escape.
Call it her captivation.
Call it her reality.
This traveler knows how to lose herself.
She knows how to find herself.
She knows how to be herself.

September 2022

~121~
Epitaph

Though I didn't want
to leave you, I remembered,
love lives forever.

Maybe goals weren't reached,
all hopes and dreams and stars, but
love lives forever.

Time has come to join
Mom, Dad and both my grands. Their
love lives forever.

When you think of me
as I always thought of them,
love lives forever.

Mourners do not weep.
Be comforted by these words:
Love lives forever.

Friends and family,
I'm in you and you're in me.
Love lives forever.

Dearly beloved,
my essence swirls around you.
Love lives forever.

Take comfort and know
I leave you all that I am.
Love lives forever.

JS.D.

March 2017

Appendix

Prologue 1
An introduction and an explanation for this book.

The Owl 2
Personal poem written for grandson Evrhett's high school graduation. Presented with a stuffed owl.

The Lion 3
Personal poem written for grandson Kohlfield's high school graduation. Presented with a stuffed lion. This was when I began to think I would like to write poetry as a way for my descendants to know me, who I am, and what I think of the world around me.

Eleven Years and Fifty Days.. 4
Personal poem written for my sister Christine commemorating our youth as we grew up together. Today our lives are distant in many ways, yet in all ways the love binds.

Clouds.. 7
First non-gift poem I wrote. Inspiration came after explaining to Christine how I was thinking of writing poetry. She asked if I would write one for her. Thus, came *Clouds* to help us deal with the loss of our mother.

Life, the Universe and Everything – Philosophical........................ 8

Life, the Universe and Everything – Personal................................ 11
These are for my friend Jeannette Stiteler. She was the inspiration for the title of these poems. A favorite phrase she often used to answer unanswerable questions back in the day. (From the book by Douglas Adams)

Tinkle Bell.. 12
Personal poem I wrote for my sister Jacqui.

God's Favorite 15
Poem I was inspired to write by Jacqui's love of animals.

Party Time.. 18
I love clichés yet they are forbidden. The rebel in me began thinking about food clichés.

Sonnet to the Clouds 20
An experiment to see if I liked 'Clouds' better if written in the more formal format of a sonnet.

Wonderful Time.. 23
The idea came to me in a dream. I just woke up with it my head. I don't know what inspired it. However, I do completely embrace it.

Pain's Prayer... 25
I am often in a lot of pain. One day I just wrote down exactly how I was feeling at that moment. Probably not exactly a poem. More a prayer, I guess.

The Villain... 27
A sonnet formatted poem I wrote as an entry to a contest at my work at SUNY Upstate Medical University. However, it did not win anything.

February Dreaming 29
Every February I dream of spring and gardening. In February I feel I can accomplish every garden task I might dream up. This poem comes from that.

Sensing Spring 31
Did I mention I long for spring every year? Here is another that helps me to deal with that longing.

Longing for Spring.. 33
I think I might have mentioned my longing for spring. Still there. I finally just put my longing into the title as well as the poem itself.

Rejuvenation.. 34
I really truly love bubble baths. I love them enough to write about how important they are and how they make me feel.

Sequel to the Owl.. 36
Personal poem for my grandson Evrhett when he graduated from college. A sequel to the original owl poem I wrote for him.

My Decades Journal.. 38
A summary of my take on each of the decades that I have been alive.

Tis the Season 40
I started to write about failing memory, but it turned into something else, an IRS poem, of all things! A commentary on my pack rat tendencies to store the happenings of each year and how satisfied I was many years later that I still had those recordings of my youth.

Sweet Home 42
We moved into my mom's home of many years on Dorwin Ave. It had grown just as worn down and ill as Mom had become over the years. Here I am expressing my feelings about why I needed to renovate the old family home and how important it was not to lose it.

Anticipation 44
One warm spring day I was grumpily thinking about how hot the weather was when I realized how easy it is to complain. I took that thought into a more emphatic, hyperbolic form.

Old Fashioned Summer 46
I still remember the summers of my youth. Now I will always have this poem when I feel my memories fading.

Remembered Freedom 49
I try to capture the feelings I have during those early days of summer, both now, and when I was a child on the last day of school. I feel the freedom, the endless possibilities.

For Alex 50
Personal poem I wrote for my grandson Alex to commemorate his sixth-grade graduation. I wasn't positive I would be here to write one for high school and college as I did for Evrhett and Kohlfield.

Truth Denied 51
I wrote this piece to help me deal with my emotions during the 2016 presidential campaign. I must remind myself that I am just one tiny cog of this country's populace. We do not all have the same beliefs. If the majority believe differently, I guess their beliefs should take precedence over mine on how our country should be run.

Highway Wonder 52
When I was quite young, I discovered a truly magical place to my childish eyes. Here, I try to capture the feelings I had when I stumbled upon the unexpected. Sadly, this place no longer exists.

The Odyssey 55
My husband Ray and I take a walk on almost every day the weather allows. It felt necessary to convey the sense of satisfaction and accomplishment we feel before, during and after the walk and how essential the walk is to our wellbeing.

Contemplating Energy 56
I was sitting in a chair just contemplating things, trying to push myself to write. If not that, at least to do something. Sometimes I get into a situation where all I do is sit around and think about nothing in particular. A little of that is okay but it is easy to get into the bad habit of doing nothing.

The Fulfillment of Beauty 58
I was wishing for a fountain in my backyard to complement my garden and invite in the beautiful birds. When my wish was fulfilled, I feared the birds would never come. Finally, they did.

Monster Within 61
Ever since I was small, maybe as young as five or six, I would imagine bad things in my bedroom or really in my head. When I was small it was usually witches or devils. As I got older the monsters became more sophisticated, but they were always there. It seems my writing may have exorcised the phenomenon to a large extent. An advantage I never anticipated.

Changing of the Guard 62
I have always said that I cannot wait for autonomous cars. I hate to drive. I am afraid of going off into a trance. I am afraid of reacting badly in an emergency. I also don't trust that others on the road will drive carefully. I cannot wait for these cars to be on the road.

Happy Birthday 63
This is an experiment using the syllables and beat of the happy birthday song in a discussion of my social beliefs.

Seeds of Time 65
Another poem that started out about memory and turned into something else. Methuselah is a tree that is supposedly the oldest in the world. It has been kept hidden for protection. I am not sure we would have civilization if we didn't have trees.

Save the Mouse 66
I feel strongly about how some people seem to be less important than even the most insignificant animal. Indifference to injustice and pain seems to run rampant in our society. It is beyond my comprehension.

The Written Word 68
Everything about books, libraries and publishing fascinate me since I enjoy reading so much.

Rain of Tears 69
Every night we see on the news the consequences of weather in our country and the world. It is awful to see the havoc wreaked by weather, how devastating to the people. The extreme destruction stays in memory for decades, if not centuries. I can only imagine the relief when good weather finally returns. It is so easy to take our beautiful, calm days for granted unless we are one of those who have known the other.

Lake 71
A sparkling, clean lake is special. I have more experience with lakes than with rivers, oceans, or mountains since I have been around them my whole life.

On Fire 73
I wrote this poem for my nephew John in celebration of his Confirmation Day.

Family Circle 74
I believe every atom of humanity has its own place in the universe. We all belong to it, and love is an integral part of that belonging.

Magic Chef 77
We go out to eat a lot. I think it is amazing that there are so many places you can go where they will feed you, fulfilling a basic need.

Fireworks Finale 79
This is about those beautiful fall days, especially when there is still some warmth in the air. Everything is bright and golden and ephemeral. Enjoy it while it lasts.

Present Participles of Love 80
Personal poem I wrote for my sister Jayne and her husband Gary for their twenty-fifth wedding anniversary. I tried to avoid the triteness of the common drivel of marital celebration, thus the present participles in italics.

Lost in a Dream – Part 1 81
This is the first in a series I wrote about dreaming. It relates a dream I have on a regular basis.

Dream Zones – Part 2 82
In the second of my dream series, I attempt to capture the frustration of waking before a sweet dream ends. Trying to recapture it, to go back inside the dream.

Dream Need – Part 3 83
The third of my dream series talks about a dream from my imagination. I imagine myself upset in a dream (needing to scream) and then stopping to think about what I am doing. All in a dream.

Last Night's Dream – Part 4 84
Here I present a collage of different dreams I have had.

Daydreaming Question – Part 5 85
As I contemplated dreams, I remembered the concept of daydreaming. We all do it and I believe it is a good thing. It is a means of determining what we wish for in life. They can also be the impetus to achieve that wish.

Dream Wisdom – Part 6 86
Some more on my thoughts about dreams. This time I put it into a more formal sonnet format. I am always curious how using fixed formats affect what I am trying to say.

What I Said 87
A long time ago when I was about twelve or thirteen years old, I was gossiping with my friend as we walked home from school. It turns out the girl I was talking about was right behind me. I felt terrible. I didn't really get an opportunity to apologize because she avoided me from then on. However, I learned a valuable lesson that day I have never forgotten.

The World's Come to This 89
Writing is a coping mechanism for me. I have no control over the terrible things I see and hear about each day. Getting my thoughts on paper is how I deal with my lack of control. Sometimes things seem very bleak.

No Hereafter 90
I know of four belief systems for what happens after we die. I give equal value to all. At different times I find myself subscribing to the validity of any of them. In the first you no longer exist after you die. Nothing more. You are done. I hope it is obvious when you read this, that I find it the hardest to accept.

Hereafter We Go Again 91
Here we explore reincarnation.

Hereafter Here 93
We look at the possibility of ghosts, goblins, vampires, and other beings who never die.

Heavenly Hereafter 94
Last of all is the traditional Judeo-Christian concept of heaven in sonnet form.

Palm Tree 97
We have gone to Florida in January from 2012-2019. I observed all kinds of palm trees there. I felt moved to celebrate their beauty and specialness.

Winter's Deadly Beauty 99
Winter is long and harsh where I live. It can be breathtakingly beautiful. But the deadliness is inherent.

The Double Sunshine 100
Again, when we go to Florida, we take a tour boat called the Double Sunshine, an experience both boring and amazing. There are the open seas, the birds, the dolphins, the music. Yet there is also the captain with his microphone droning on about the rich and famous.

Fate's Fortune 102
There are times I think about and realize how blessed I am, all the privileges I take for granted. Probably most in the world could not even imagine.

Sad Psyche 105
I hate that this probably makes me sound like a huge whiner. However, since the purpose of my writing is so that you may know me, I find it necessary. It is a big part of who I am. I have had high anxiety/panic issues for as long as I can remember.

Pious Passion 106
A little satire to help me deal with the world we live in, with the haves and the have nots. The overwhelming idea is that the haves deserve everything they have because they "worked hard" for it. The have nots obviously do not deserve anything. Pray for them and you have done your part (sarcasm).

Serving King Tomorrow 107
I worked at SUNY Upstate Medical University for more than fifty years. This poem pays tribute to the work I did there.

Picture Frame of Life.. 109

On August 20, 2014, I took a fall from the front steps of Dorwin Ave. I broke both my arms and my left knee. I spent a month in a nursing home, then came home to recuperate. I was not very mobile. I spent most of my time in bed looking out the window. Here I try to convey how I felt at that time.

Journey to Destiny 110

Personal poem I wrote for my grandson Kohlfield on his graduation from college. It is the sequel to the one I wrote at high school graduation (The Lion).

Weed Worthy 113

I love to garden. I spend a lot of time weeding.

Face It... 114

Writing about it was a way to deal with disappointment when I failed to get any recognition in a contest I entered. A bit of hyperbole perhaps, yet not really. It is very hard to accept your own mediocrity.

La-La Land 115

After I fell in August 2014, I was on opioids for quite a long time. I still have some of those pills saved for times when I am in extreme pain. I don't think I am addicted. I go months, even years without taking one. But then one day, I will decide I can't take it anymore, and I will take one of these pills.

Paths.. 117

Here I write of a time when I realized I could have done something differently. I wanted to start over again, try a new way that might lead back to the old beginning. The old beginning was desirable. The path I chose was not. I want to undo the wrong path and try again.

Slippers 118

I have had pain, well, not exactly pain, but perhaps a freezing cold numbness in both of my feet for a very long time. One day I got new slippers which I loved. Before they finally wore down, they made my feet feel warm and cozy and comfortable. It might not sound like a big deal, but for me it allowed a much more positive outlook on life.

Modern Art.. 121

Here I try to make some sense of art when I have no idea what it might mean.

Goodbye 122

Saying goodbye is always difficult no matter the circumstances. Short and to the point (though still so very painful) might be best. This is any kind of goodbye you can imagine.

Dining Room Table 125
Sometimes I just think about things. I will look at my table and wonder where it will be one hundred years from now. It is a good table. I hope it is still in use.

Deep 126
I was pondering about the word "Deep," with all its connotations. I was moved to try to express my thoughts.

Tiny Bits 129
Things may not always go as you would like. Life can be difficult. However, always, if you look, there are those little bits waiting to give you pleasure.

I Never Met Him 130
My friend's brother died. Though I never met him I always heard about him. I was so impressed by what he was trying to accomplish in his life.

I Said So 131
What can I say? This is just true. Human nature, I guess. It is kind of funny, but distressing, nevertheless.

Almost Here 133
Remember me longing for spring? Well, now I am longing for summer. Maybe spring was wet and cold. I just needed to remind myself that the lilacs and peonies would eventually bloom. The wedding and graduation season would come as always. This is the time of year which creates the most forever memories.

Symphony Refrained 135
Music has always been a fundamental need in my life. I think that might be universal.

Puddle Jumping 136
Rainy summer days of my childhood we would go out in our bathing suits and run through the rain and jump in the puddles. I can remember how that made me feel to this day.

I See You 137
I am reminded how you can see your loved ones every day but not really know them. Sometimes something special will happen and your eyes will be opened and the world as you knew it will have changed.

State of Mine 138
An entry to a contest at the New York State Fair. It was required to be about New York State, its fair, or its symbols. I received an "Honorable Mention."

Cliché 140
Here I explore the pros and cons of clichés. They became so because they were usually clever and useful. So hard not to use them because I almost always like them.

Tattooed Gardener 142
Gardening memories from my youth have directly led to my current infatuation with gardening. The memories are like tattoos, indelible, forever.

Sunset on a Florida Beach 145
On our annual sojourn to Florida one of my most favorite experiences was the sunset. The emotions I felt are indescribable but still I tried.

Sixteen 147
Personal poem written for my niece Jill for her sixteenth birthday.

Once Upon a Time 148
I finally get closer to the problems with memory often experienced as you get older. The fear of dementia and/or Alzheimer's is very real.

Life's Delight 150
Music is the one of the most amazing things. I cannot imagine our world without it.

My Personal Awe's List 153
Maybe you could call this a "poetical list." I thought if you want to know me then you should know those things which I consider most awesome.

Magnolia Bush 157
Personal poem I wrote for my daughter Becky and her family. She has a beautiful magnolia tree in front of her house where the hummingbirds like to hang out.

Age-Old Resolution 158
At the time of the new year, our thoughts often go to diet and exercise. The need for these grows more interesting and possibly more desperate the older you get.

Lady Bountiful 159
She just came out of my imagination. A fantasy who possessed my idea of perfect outer beauty. I would love to have known her. Perhaps I would have loved to have been her.

Fear of Fire..160
Just as I thought you should know what I consider awesome, I thought it necessary to write about my deepest fear. One I have had since I was not much older than a toddler.

It's All Good..162
Life is an adventure. Often there are many hardships to overcome. There is wonder in how the ending might turn out.

Honor...164
This is not about heroes or warriors or saviors of any kind. Just what it means to be an honorable person every day.

Hermit Crab..165
We used to have one of these as a pet. I researched the environment they love – in the sand next to the sea. I can identify with these creatures in many ways. Neither of us are really hermits though sometimes it might feel as if we are.

The Travelers...166
Everywhere you look, you will see people on the smart phones, myself and Ray included. I would love to travel more but doubt I ever will again. I suppose this is another way to fulfill that need. People watching is also a favorite occupation of ours, and for many others as well.

Back Seat Driver...168
A woman nagging her husband in the car is the comical stereotype of a backseat driver. I am she, but I assure you there is no comical relief intended here. This is the story of what it means to be anxiety-driven. Never feeling safe. Ruled by fear. Never wanting to leave home.

This New Spring 171
In my mind the Covid-19 virus and the coming of spring are forever intertwined. Our first reactions in this country started in early March 2020. Spring no longer had the meaning it held in the past. It is hard to appreciate the rebirth of the earth when death seems to be all around you.

Still… 172
There are so many sides to all of us…. It is interesting what we choose to hide.

Uneasy 173
Once when I was contemplating the world where I currently reside, I had this strong feeling of uneasiness. It was so overpowering I felt driven to capture my state of mind at that time.

Congratulations 174
For my nephew and his wife upon the birth of their first child.

Animal Shelter 175
Contemplating animal shelters but also the human condition (shelters, zoos, nursing homes, hospitals, refugee camps, prisons… schools, work, life!)

Play Ball 176
My entry for grandson Alex's high school yearbook. Life advice.

Memories of Mom 177
Bits of memories I have of my years of life with my mom, with a nod to Paul Lawrence Dunbar's "Beyond the Years." Lillian Corinne Hunt Scannell Wenborne 1925 – 2013.

The Western Sky 183
Experimental writing giving homage to a song I love, "Bridge Over Troubled Water" by Simon and Garfunkel. Life lessons on learning and living, within the confines of my seventy-plus-year-old mind.

Pillow Talk 184
The murmurings of a couple just before sleep overtakes them.

Curiosity 186
There are so many interesting things in life if you just take the time to appreciate them. It's amazing where curiosity will lead, sometimes the happiness and contentment of a new hobby, sometimes a life-changing moment.

Gulliver 187
Travel and reading – true escapes from the real world. For many, myself included, essential for sanity.

The Wolf 188
Poem dedicated to my grandson Alex upon high school graduation. His "spirit animal" in a lot of ways, I have often thought.

Light the Way 189
A tribute to teachers, in particular, my sister Jayne. (With a nod to "Rock-a-bye Baby" because Jayne is my baby sister after all.)

Listen, Listen, Maestro Man 190
A tribute to my son Tim Davis whose love of music and caring for his students have changed the lives of many for the better. (With a nod to "Twinkle, Twinkle, Little Star," one of the first pieces a budding musician will learn.)

Blank Slate 191
This is inspired from my addiction to sudoku puzzles. However, even as I do them, I can't believe how closely it resembles starting anything new: a job, a project, marriage, parenthood, life. The idea of starting over, writing your own destiny.

Standing Engagement 193
A modified Japanese tanka. My love and awe for the performance of nature every year.

An Ocean of Tears 195
I cry very easily, over many things. I sometimes think my tears might fill an ocean.

Big Box 196
Walmart, Amazon, Lowes, Target, Home Depot…

Clean House 197
We have lived in four newly built homes and three older homes. The one we currently live in was built in 1927. My mother lived here for forty-five years before us. I do know of that which I speak.

Tribute to the Peony 199
A lovely plant that can live one hundred years or more! It was Uncles Bill's favorite. We did plant one on his grave.

Awakenings 200
Turning points in life. Choices that change us forever.

Imagination's Tutor 203
Reading is wondrous. The world is yours. You will learn who you are.

Epitaph 204
A series of haikus. Just as the title says, it is my epitaph for my life and the epilogue for this book.

About the Author

JoAnne Davis was born, raised, and educated in Syracuse New York. She graduated from Syracuse University with a BS in Information Systems. She worked at SUNY Upstate Medical University for over fifty years, starting as a keypunch operator, advancing over the years to become assistant director to her department. During this time, she and her husband also raised a son and a daughter. She currently resides in Syracuse with her husband, Ray. As an avid, voracious reader, who always wanted to try her hand at writing herself, this was her chance.

JoAnne is eager to communicate with anyone interested in discussing her work. Her email is davisjoannescannell@gmail.com. She is currently working on developing a web presence at jsdlegacy.com.

Printed in the USA
CPSIA information can be obtained
at www.ICGtesting.com
LVHW060337220524
780921LV00010B/63